EMERGING MONEY MARKET IN INDIA

EMERGING MONEY MARKET IN INDIA

Edited by

ALAK GHOSH

DEEP & DEEP PUBLICATIONS PVT. LTD.

F-159, Rajouri Garden, New Delhi - 110 027

First Published : 2001
Reprinted : 2004

ISBN 81-7629-267-2

Typeset by LASER TECH, A-31A, Rajouri Garden,
New Delhi-110 027 • Phones : 25930798, 25469995

Printed in India by ELEGANT PRINTERS,
A-38/2, Mayapuri Industrial Area, Phase-I, New Delhi-110 064.

Published by DEEP & DEEP PUBLICATIONS PVT. LTD.,
F-159, Rajouri Garden, New Delhi - 110 027
Phones : 25435369, 25440916
E-mails : ddpbooks@yahoo.co.in • deep98@del3.vsnl.net.in
Showroom :
2/13, Ansari Road, Daryaganj, New Delhi -110 002 • Telefax : 23245122

Contents

Foreword ix

Preface xi

Introduction xiii

List of Contributors xix

PART A
GENERAL OBSERVATIONS

1. *M.G. Bhide*
Emerging Money Market in India 3

2. *Dev Raj*
Functioning of Money Market in a Market Economy with Reference to India 17

3. *Deepak Mohanty and Argya Kusum Mitra*
Evolution of Money Markets in India 45

PART B
MONEY AND CAPITAL MARKET INTERACTIONS

4. *T.V.S. Rammohan Rao*
Stock Market Adjustments to Policy Changes 61

5. *A.J. Chakraborty*
Capital Market in India—The Role of Commercial Banks 75

6. *Sanjib Chandra Basu and Subodh Chandra Garai*
Long-run Behaviour of Indian Money Market : A Spectral Analysis of Call Money Rate 86

PART C
RURAL MONEY MARKETS

7. *V.B. Jugale*
Implications of Structural Reforms on Rural Money Market 101

8. *Gian Kaur and Anita Gill*
Nature and Extent of Interlinkage of Agrarian Credit Markets : A Case of Punjab 114

PART D
INDIAN MONEY MARKET UNDER ECONOMIC REFORMS

9. *V.N. Attri and Neera Verma*
Emerging Money Market in India under Economic Reforms: The Need for Integration with Foreign Exchange Market 137

10. *Vijay Laxmi Chari*
Money Market Instruments : The Case of Certificate of Deposit 151

PART E
TRANSFORMATION OF INDIAN MONEY MARKET AND FURTHER REFORMS

11. *Tuli Roy and V. Upadhyay*
Recent Changes in Money Market—Some Suggestions for Further Reforms 167

12. *B.K. Bhoi*
Emerging Money Market in India: Agenda for Further Reforms 176

13. *Amalesh Banerjee and Pratul Chatterjee*
Transformation of Indian Money Market—Which Way? 196

Index 208

Foreword

Right from Kautilya's Artha Sastra to the writings of the great stalwarts of the nineteenth century—Raja Ram Mohan Roy, G.V. Joshi, Dadabhai Naoroji, Romesh Chandra Dutt and Gopal Krishna Gokhale, India has been contributing significantly to the Economics, but professionalism in the discipline was absent till 1909, when Calcutta University prescribed a separate honours course in Economics. An M.A. course in the subject, delinked from the other social sciences was started a year later by the University. The major universities in India followed suit.

Professor C.J. Hamilton, Minto Professor of Political Economy, Calcutta University convened a provided the spring board for the formation of the Indian Economics Association to promote the study, teaching and research in Economics in general and Indian economy in particular. The formal conference of the Association was held at Bombay in December 1918 under presidentship of Professor Percy Anstey. Since then the Association has been serving the profession and discipline through holding regular annual conferences, national and regional seminars, workshops and Round Tables in different parts of the country. The Association has been publishing regularly Journal, Conference Volume and other materials. All these have immensely contributed to the maturity of the profession and the development of the discipline. The present volume is an effort in this direction.

The papers included in the volume were discussed during the Hyderabad conference of the Indian Economic Association, held in the month of December 1997. An organised money market provided an efficient mechanism for the transmission of the monetary regulation to the rest of the economy. Substantial changes have been made in the Indian money market during

Post Sukhamoy Chakravarty Committee Report especially economic reforms to obtain the efficient mechanism in the system. The authors have evaluated the different dimensions of the theme with pragmatic considerations.

I would like to place on record our gratitude to Prof. Alak Ghosh for editing the papers and preparing a useful introduction. I express my gratitude to Dr. Amalesh Banerjee, Vice President, IEA, Dr. Raj Kumar Sen, Secretary & Treasurer, IEA and Dr. P.R. Brahmananda, Managing Editor, IEJ for their active cooperation in publication of the book. Mr. G.S. Bhatia, Deep & Deep Publications Pvt. Ltd. deserves special mention and gratitude for publication of the book within stipulated time frame.

In view of importance of the theme with policy significance the book may help the policy makers, embattled executives, other practitioners and academicians.

AJIT KUMAR SINHA
President
Indian Economic Association

Preface

The Indian Economic Association (IEA), in its 80th year of academic activities, decided to publish themewise edited volumes out of papers contributed to IEA Annual Conferences during 1994-2000. A number of such titles are now under publication. *Emerging Money Market in India* is one of such edited volumes containing as many as 13 articles and grouped under five sub-themes, viz. General Observations; Money and Capital Market Interactions; Rural Money Markets; Indian Money Market under Economic Reforms; Transformation of Indian Money Market and Further Responses. The major contributions of these articles are available in a summarised form in the Introduction which follows. We sincerely hope that the readers will find the contents of this volume both light and fruit bearing.

We are thankful to Dr. G.S. Monga, our former President for his positive contributions to make this publication programme a reality. Thanks are also due to Prof. Ajit Kumar Sinha, President, IEA for his Foreword and interest. We thank all the contributors and the editor of this volume without whose cooperation, this volume could not be published. Last but not the least we thank Deep & Deep Publications Pvt. Ltd. for its cooperation and help to publish this and other volumes in this series in record time and elegant manner. We also apologise to our members for any of the lapses that may remain in these volumes for reasons beyond our control.

Calcutta

RAJ KUMAR SEN
Managing Editor

Introduction

India has witnessed in the past two decades substantial changes in the money and capital markets. The money market scenario, which has emerged since 1980s, has witnessed new instruments and new directions have been chalked out. It is to be noted here that, strictly speaking, the money market deals with short-term flow of funds whereas the capital market, embracing the stock market, deals with medium and long-term capital flows. But these two markets can not be placed in water-tight compartments and there is often a spillover from one market to the other. This explains why the papers included in this volume not only deal with money market problems but also with issues arising out of the growth and working of the Indian capital market. However, it is pertinent to note that the main thrust of the papers, presented in this volume, is on the issues connected with the emerging role of the Indian money market in a market-economy setting.

The first of three papers, by M.G. Bhide deals with evolution and general functioning of money markets in India. Bhide, after discussing various aspects of the functioning and growth of the Indian money market, suggests the setting up of a Central Settlement Agency by the RBI which will neutralise the frictions in the market. Dev Raj with some excellent charts and diagrams, has shown the structural framework of money and capital markets. However, his emphasis is more on the functioning of the capital market than on the money market. Deepak Mohanty and A.K. Mitra in their paper have provided a systematic review of the evolution of the money market in India. They have shown that, in recent years, the bank rate is serving as a 'signalling rate' so as to influence market behaviour. They have also shown that in the emerging Indian money market a growing inter-linkage has developed between the domestic money market and the forex market.

The second set of three papers deals with money and capital market interaction-short and long-run behaviours. The paper by T.V.S. Rammohan Rao deals with both the primary and secondary sectors of the capital market. Rao believes that steady trends in stock prices can be achieved only if there are tangible investments in infrastructure industries and basic consumer goods industries. However, the problem is not that easy in the face of unexpected pulls and pressures coming from within and outside. A.J. Chakrabarty in his paper deals in detail the capital markets and the role of commercial banks. The author examines the role of mainly public sector banks as an intermediary in the capital market. The author firmly believes that the Indian commercial banking system cannot act as the most important intermediary in the Indian capital market unless the unfinished agenda of financial reforms is seriously implemented within a short period of time. Sanjib Chandra Basu and Subodh Chandra Garai have presented a very interesting spectral analysis of the call money rate. It is to be noted here that in India the inter-bank call money market formed the core of money market till the late 1980s. Since then the Indian money market has been undergoing systematic proliferation and diversification. In the emerging money market many new instruments have cropped up. But all these developments have not undermined the role of the call money rate. Today, call money market is gradually emerging as the focal point for Central Bank intervention for influencing liquidity in the Indian economy. Basu and Garai have made a systematic study, with statistical tools, of the behaviour of the call-money rate in India for a long period covering both pre- and post-liberalisation eras. This analysis throws new light on the problem dealing with fluctuations in the call-money rate.

There are two papers dealing with rural money markets. The first paper by V.V. Jugale shows the impact of structural reforms on rural money markets. Jugale is of the opinion that the large-scale agro-business will emerge in the near future as a result of economic reforms. In this new scenario, Jugale believes that NGOs will have to play a more effective role and they will ultimately outstrip the rural co-operatives. It is pertinent to note here that the "Gramin Banks" are now effectively transforming the agrarian credit market in Bangladesh. Jugale could have drawn lessons from Bangladeshi Gramin Bank experiment. The second paper in this group by Gian Kaur and Anita Gill has analysed the nature and extent of interlinkage in the informal credit market of a specific rural-dominated region of Punjab. Kaur and Gill show that in the informal credit market in Patiala more than 80% of the households obtain credit through linked transactions. It is interesting to note that inter-linkage increases with increase in the size of holdings. This is certainly a startling revelation. The authors suggest a pragmatic solution for increasing the availability of rural credit. They are bold enough to recommend that interest rates charged by the formal institutions in rural areas may be freed.

In the next two papers the authors discuss two special aspects of emerging money market in India under economic reforms. The first paper by V.N. Attri and Neera Verma tries to establish the relationships between Indian money market and foreign-exchange market. The main conclusion of the authors is that the growth rates would have been higher and faster, if a market-oriented and active foreign exchange policy was persued together with positive monetary policy. Attri and Verma believe that market-determined interest rates can become an effective instrument in controlling the volatile nature of foreign-exchange market under floating exchange rate policy. The next paper by Ms. Vijay Laxmi Chari deals with case of Certificate of Deposit (CD) in the emerging Indian money market. It should be remembered that the return on CDs is usually determined by the prevailing rates in the call-money market. CD is popular instrument in the New York money market but has lost its importance in the London money market. It was introduced in India in 1990. During the first few years this instrument was quite popular as the call money rates were very high and volatile but, with further liberalisation of money market as a consequence of economic reforms, the call money rates started to settle down at lower levels, the importance of CDs gradually declined and commercial papers gained the upper-hand. Chari would like to change the method of trading in CDs so as to make them more popular. Considering that CDs usually carry less risk than inter-corporate deposits, they may become more popular with the spread in money market operations to centres such as Chennai, Calcutta and Ahmedabad. It is a pity that Chari does not fully spell out the policy.

The next set of three papers discusses the transformation of Indian money market and give suggestions for further reforms. The first paper by Tuli Roy and V. Upadhyaya analyses the changes that have been brought about in existing money market instruments and also list some of the new instruments that have gained prominence in the post-reform era. These include introduction of 14 day Treasury Bills, Money Market Mutual Funds, setting up of Primary Dealers, DFHI, (Discount and Finance House of India) and STCI (Securities Trading Corporation of India). These changes have substantially helped in deepening and widening the money market. However, to remove some deficiencies the authors suggest the introduction of foreign currency money market instruments and want to increase the scope of satellite dealers in the money markets. The next paper by B.K. Bhoi, after discussing the general environment in which the Indian money market operates, goes on to describe the developments in the government securities' market as it is regarded as an integral part of the money market. Bhoi comes to the agenda for further reforms. His suggestions are bold, innovative and pragmatic. He is of the view that exchange rate, as far as practicable, should be market-determined. Intervention, if necessary, should be made in the forward market. More important point to note here is that intervention in the forex market requires to be synchronised with money market intervention. Another suggestion of Bhoi is that corporates may be allowed to float CPs as an additional channel of financing their working capital requirements. The lock-in-periods of CPs and CDs may be initially reduced to 15 days and completely withdrawn at an appropriate time. These and other innovative suggestions from a practising banker enhance the quality of the paper. Last but not least this volume also includes in article by Amalesh Banerjee and Pratul Chatterjee. According to them, the process of financial widening and deepening have brought about a plethora of weak finance companies which, in most cases, have put black-spots on the emerging money market fabric. They also give a clarion call for the immediate revamping and reorganising of the rural financial structure so that effective institutions and instruments are developed to channelise sufficient funds to wider activities which encompass rural areas. Banerjee and Chatterjee believe that here the government is destined to play a significant role. Under the regime of liberalisation, the RBI and the government should jointly play the role of an effective facilitator for redirection of fund flows between competitive financial institutions.

In conclusion, we have to note that the Indian Capital market in recent years has served as a major vehicle of economic growth. With the opening up of the Indian economy, consequent upon the economic reforms, the Indian Capital market witnessed unprecedented euphoria in the early nineties and helped the globalisation process. It is destined to bring about a closer integration of domestic capital market with global market through greater involvement of FIIs and foreign private investors (including NRIs). Indian monetory policy during the nineties, which suffered from *ad-hocism*, could not make much positive contribution to the process of fully activating the money market. Unfortunataly, the RBI was more concerned in maintaining exchange rate stability and neglected its twin task of monetary stability and money market development.

ALAK GHOSH

List of Contributors

Prof. Ajit Kumar Sinha, President, IEA.

Dr. Raj Kumar Sen, Secretary and Treasurer, IEA.

Prof. Alak Ghosh, Former President (1987), IEA.

Shri M.G. Bhide, Indian Overseas Bank, Mumbai.

Dr. Dev Raj, Bank of Baroda, New Delhi.

Shri Deepak Mohanty, DEAP, Reserve Bank of India, Mumbai.

Shri Argya Kusum Mitra, DEAP, Reserve Bank of India, Mumbai.

Prof. T.V.S. Rammohan Rao, Indian Institute of Technology, Kanpur.

Shri A.J. Chakraborty, Calcutta.

Shri Sanjib Chandra Basu, K.K. Das College of Commerce, Calcutta.

Dr. Subodh Chandra Garai, K.K. Das College of Commerce, Calcutta.

Dr. V.B. Jugale, V.M. National Institute of Cooperative Management, Pune.

Dr. Gian Kaur, Guru Nanak Dev University, Amritsar.

Dr. Anita Gill, Punjab University, Amritsar.

Dr. V.N. Attri, Kurukshetra University, Haryana.

Smt. Neera Verma, Kurukshetra, Haryana.

Dr. Vijay Laxmi Chari, Gujarat University, Ahmedabad.

Smt. Tuli Roy, Reserve Bank of India, New Delhi.

Dr. V. Upadhyay, Indian Institute of Technology, New Delhi.

Shri B.K. Bhoi, DEAP, Reserve Bank of India, Mumbai.

Prof. Amalesh Banerjee, Rabindra Bharati University, Calcutta.

Dr. Pratul Chatterjee, B.K.C. College (Retd.), Calcutta.

List of Contributors

PART A

GENERAL OBSERVATIONS

1

Emerging Money Market in India

M.G. BHIDE

It is an emerging money market in India, since till recently, money market was operating in a regulated interest rate environment. The interest rates were perceived to be means of reallocation of resources and hence did not reflect true supply and demand position in the market. It is pertinent to note that even when RBI did not control the call money rates, IBA for some time had stipulated a ceiling over the rates, since interest rates on deposits and credit were otherwise controlled by RBI. As a result, money market was essentially an interbank market, to facilitate exchange of funds at marginal level, i.e. only in the context of surplus or shortfall in liquidity.

Today, money is a cashflow with a high velocity flowing into the hands of users willing and able to pay the right price. The money market is providing essential liquidity to the economic system, not only to the banks, but to all the issuers and investors (borrowers and lenders) connected to the market. This has been possible as there are more players and more instruments to play with, in the market place.

The factors which helped induce dynamism into the market are deregulation of inerest rate and greater integration of markets, with corporates and institutional investors as new players.

Money market, in its narrow sense, is confined to banking and financial institutions, who maintain an account with the Central Bank. However, money market in reality consists of all dealings involving cash and near cash assets, and short-term investment paper (with maturities shorter than 1 year, as per convention). The Central Bank also uses money market for liquidity management through its open market operations. Apart from banks and financial institutions, the other players in the market include foreign institutional investors, mutual funds and corporates. Thus, the money market engulfs in part or full, treasuries, corporate debt and private investment areas. The instruments that circulate in money market are treasury bills, certificates of deposits, commercial paper, acceptances, repurchases agreements, and pronotes—all of which are essentially negotiable.

Financial markets are, for ease of reference, divided into four sectors, viz. money markets, capital market, securities market and foreign exchange market. These markets are intertwined and are mutually interacting, but get segregated and hence become less efficient if : (a) there are restrictions on players, (b) the securities are not easily negotiable, (c) the currency is not convertible, or (d) there is no depth in the market for a variety of reasons, (such as the debt issue is of small size, there are no market makers, or there is no proper settlement system). If these hurdles are removed, there would be greater interaction between the market forces and the investment flows freely across the sectors. The linkages develop between short-term and long-term interest rates, between domestic and foreign rates of interest, and between return on debt and equity. Any sector movement of funds results in a cash flow which is part of money market, and an efficient money market reallocates the investment to different alernatives available in all these sectors. For instance, in a free economy, if the stock index goes up, the currency will appreciate, which pushes up short-term interest rates which, in turn, would lead to a fall in bond prices.

Sectoral readjustment of investible funds implies an exchange of risks and as the investments grow to be rate sensitive, hedging mechanism becomes an essential ingredient of financial markets. A currency swap, for example, would help to avail of higher rates of interest in another currency without exposing to exchange risk.

The function of money market is therefore to provide liquidity to the system by means of : (a) access to cash and cash equivalent assets, (b) ease of shifting from fixed assets to current assets and from current assets to cash at market determined rates, and (c) risk management (to provide for risk in exchanging cashflows). Though not strictly part of money market, mortgage securities (asset securitisation), secondary market for syndication loans, leasing and factoring services help to enhance liquidity in the system and hence form different layers of the same market.

Banks are most important players in money market because of their unique presence in all the market segments, and their command over resources. Banks provide financial intermediation (credit risk) and maturity intermediation (mismatch risk), besides providing a payment mechanism. Banks traditionally absorb and redistribute risk by diversification in the credit and investment areas. Banks also specialize in risk management techniques, as they hold highly liquid and rate sensitive funds on behalf of deposit customers and their own shareholders.

Public policy in India has favoured more active money market so as to facilitate a more efficient liquidity management in the economy. The monetary reforms progressed in the direction of creating a more user-friendly environment and also to add depth to the money market by increasing the number of market players. Beginning with revised accounting norms introduced in the year 1992, the financial reforms policy over the years, has graduated to convertibility of Rupee on current account, removal of ceiling on lending rates, de-restricting the financial institutions and finally removing ceiling on deposit rates. The financial reforms culminated in the latest Monetary and Credit Policy of Reserve Bank of India (RBI), which entails three landmark changes: (a) Total deregulation of interest rates, (b) Drastic reduction in CRR, undeterred by high liquidity in the economy; and (c) Globalisation of Indian banks, by permitting them to commit a small but significant portion of their resources for the purposes of investment in overseas markets. The RBI, it would appear, has also endorsed, in principle, the recommendations of Committee on Capital Account Convertibility (CAC), paving the way to lift the exchange controls substantially within the next three years.

As a result, the interest rates are now market-driven and there are more players in the market including financial institutions, foreign investment institutions and mutual funds—although they are still subject to certain restrictions. Short-term debt market has also flourished with the removal of restrictions on issue of Commercial Papers by corporates and the certificates of deposits by banks. The markets have become more integrated and there is greater interaction between domestic and global markets.

The RBI, in addition to deregulation of markets has also taken affirmative action to enhance the liquidity and to widen the reach of money market. Repos have been permitted virtually on all Government securities and Banks and Institutions are free to enter into Repos or reverse Repos in all the securities. Treasury bills of 14 days and 28 days have been introduced in the market and the settlement mechanism has also improved in Government securities. The Government securities are now in paperless form and are settled on the basis of Delivery *vs.* Payment (DvP). There is also greater transparency in publication of SGL data which has helped to improve the secondary market for Government securities.

Against the background of the monetary reforms already introduced, the emergence of money market is no longer solely dependent on public policy. The RBI will henceforth assume supervisory role, rather than a regulatory role and will encourage self-regulation in the markets. The market has to evolve from within, to become more efficient.

Indian money market is still in elementary stage of development as compared to the global market. The following deficiencies can be detected at functional level:

(i) The markets are unidirectional with a few large banks and institutions determining the trend in interest rates. Despite the new entrants in the market, there are few banks who can quote two-way rates for overnight or term funds as some players are always net borrowers in the market, just as some are always net lenders in the market.

(ii) There is a felt need for benchmark interest rate, in

the absence of which, the term money market has failed to develop.

(iii) Financial Institutions, Foreign institutional investors and Money Market Mutual Funds are subject to restrictions that hamper their role in the money markets.

(iv) There is also scope to increase the number of instruments available in the money market. Repurchase Agreements, acceptances and commercial bill discounting is less common in Indian money markets as compared to global markets. There is virtually no secondary market for loan transfers, although Participation Certificates are existing in a limited way. There is no centralized settlement mechanism and almost all non-government securities are issued in physical form. Secondary market in securities has not taken off in view of bottlenecks in the settlement process, sometimes caused by tax deducted at source or stamp duty.

(v) There is no hedging mechanism available for setting off maturity and interest rate risks. The exchange risks are also covered by convention swaps and forwards, and the derivatives such as currency options have yet to become popular with corporate clients.

At the root of the above deficiencies, there lie the problems related to :

(A) Dealing and Settlement Mechanism;

(B) A Credible yield Curve; and

(C) Restrictions Placed by the Regulatory Environ.

(A) Dealing and Settlement Mechanism

As on date we have a weak dealing and settlement mechanism. Dealing is conducted over phone, both in money market and securities market, and the rates are negotiated after a lot of haggling. There are two weaknesses in the system. Firstly, it is virtually impossible for a buyer or a lender to contact all the counter parties and negotiate the best possible rates; hence the market remains imperfect. Secondly, the very presence of a major player, such as SBI or LIC is sufficient to drive the market in the direction they desire. The market thus remains unidirectional on any given day.

In my view, solution to the problem lies in screen based anonymous trading in money market, in the same way as it is done in equity markets in NSE. By networking the banks and institution that deal in money market through a satellite link, we can establish a mechanism whereby orders can be placed on the screen for borrowing/lending or for purchase/sale of debut instruments. When the right price is struck, matching of orders takes place on the screen, at which stage only, the identity of buyer and seller is disclosed. The movement in interest rates and security prices this way become more market-related and more objective.

An additional advantage of screen-based trading is that it can be expanded to cover all money centres, and a true, nation-wide money market can be created, overcoming the geographical segregation of markets. Money market at present is concentrated in Bombay and for want of access and transfer costs, the players in other important centres are not able to fully participate in the market. A nation-wide market could take care of any excess of supply and demand for funds appearing in any pocket, and hence the resulting interest rate would be truly representative of the market.

A nationally integrated market would also help Reserve Bank of India to conduct its open market operations more efficiently and would lend stronger support to secondary market in securities. Steps taken in the recent past are indicative of introduction of screen-based trading in the near future.

An efficient dealing system also presupposes an efficient settlement system. Presently, all money market settlements are by means of bankers' cheques which are physically handed over to the counter-party within the clearing hours. All security deals are also settled against transfer of physical paper. Even when Government Securities are traded in paperless form, SGL form are to be physically carried and handed over to the counter-party.

Apart from counter-party risks and inconvenience in

handling physical paper, the type of settlement system we have today is incompatiable with screen-based dealing and nation-wide money market. What we need is a centralised clearing and settlement system where funds can be transferred with same day value and securities can be on DvP basis. When banks are able to provide 'any time anywhere' banking to customer, it is not impossible that they themselves avail of similar service from a centrally constituted facility.

I feel that the Reserve Bank of India could take initiative in setting up a Central Settlement Agency, who will have four parallel functions viz.,

(a) Payment Function—automatic debits and credits to accounts of member banks and other institutional member (to be confined to banks and financial institutions).
(b) Custodial function—to hold custody of Government Securities and all eligible corporate securities (norms as to credit rating and issue size may be fixed) in D-mat form.
(c) Settlement function—instantly crediting the securities account and debiting the party account (and vice-a-versa) on DvP basis, and
(d) Lending Function—to be able to lend overnight funds (overdraft) as also securities to the member institutions as per prefixed lending limits. Securities lending constitutes an integral part of settlement function, in an actively traded securities market.

Ideally, interbank money market and security market settlement should be handled by the same agency. Custodial arrangement will be similar to the one we have with CEDEL and EUROCLEAR for global securities. A prerequisite for this function, is that all eligible securities are registered and lodged in D-mat form with the central agency, prior to commencement of trading.

The payment mechanism can be on gross or net basis. Real time gross settlement system has already been adopted in several European and Asia Pacific countries, including UK, Switzerland, Thailand, Australia and Hongkong. Net payment is day-end settlement after processing the day's transactions and is the system adopted in clearing houses. The nearest model available to us is Hongkong Monetary Authority who have successfully commenced only a few years back, security related custody and settlement services through CMU (Central Money Unit) as also RTGS for real time settlement of funds. While RTGS would be a step forward for our purpose. Reserve Bank of India may commence a similar autonomous unit for inter-bank money market and security market settlements with end-of-the day processing. While there is little counter-party risk in interbank dealings and settlements on DvP basis, it is implied that the autonomous unit will indemnify against all trade related risks.

There are also other minor hindrances for smoothening the settlement process, such as TDS (tax deducted at source) and stamp duty, applicable to certain types of securities. However, Reserve Bank and Government of India are capable of removing such obstructions, given that development of the market is a more important objective.

(B) A Credible Yield Curve

The other source of induced market distortion is absence of a yield curve. A credible yield curve would establish a term structure of interest rates, with a relationship between long-term and short-term rates and would also help evolve a bench-mark reference rate. A yield curve is also the basis for developing interest rate derivatives.

The market distortions are apparent in the high volatility of call money rate and the virtual absence of term money market (i.e. interbank lending for one week/one month/three months, etc.) The rate structure appears to be irrational in that at the shorter-end, government securities yield higher than bank deposits (whereas sovereign risk should yield the lowest) and on quite a few occasions overnight interest rates were, significantly higher than the rates available on 'AAA' rated commercial paper.

A question arises why there is no credible yield curve, despite there being a large volume of government securities (ours is the third largest bond market in Asia). The reasons are two-fold. Firstly, owing to SLR requirements, the government securities have a captive market. Till recently, the coupons were not market driven. Reserve Bank's efforts to monetise the deficit have since forced Government of India to raise public debt at market rates of interest. However, the Government Securities still have a captive market as the number of non-bank players is limited and there is also a crowding-out effect. There is no retail market as the individual buyers of securities will have settlement problems and in any case, all the securities are not readily tradeable.

Secondly, there is no short-term interbank money market. In a developing economy, long-term interest rates and increasingly driven by short-term rates. The absence of term market, is not conducive to a credible yield curve.

The interbank term market did not take off partly because of the CRR requirement. The CRR is calculated on the basis of average derived from fortnightly daily products of balances maintained in the RBI account. Banks are hence preoccupied with daily cash balances and are unable to view requirements beyond overnight placements. Volatility of call money rates is such that by depending on overnight borrowings, banks expect to either reduce their interests cost or make a profit out of it, by taking advantage of the products.

It is also true that the banks do not yet pay much attention to the Asset Liability Management, and hence any mismatch would first reflect in shortage of CRR are the banks would find the easy way out by resorting to overnight money market, unless the mismatch is quite serious enough. The Reserve Bank of India (RBI) can help to establish a market conducive yield curve by redefining the SLR requirements and by enlarging the scope of operations of non-bank dealers. For the purpose of SLR, the RBI may approve liquifiable securities other than Government Securities, i.e. corporate securities and securities denominated in foreign currency, subject to a minimum credit rating and after satisfying itself that there is an active secondary market for the instruments. I am suggesting the latter (global securities) since SLR is now applicable to FCNR Deposits and in any case, banks are also allowed to hold overseas investment to the extend of 15% of their Tier-1 capital. The RBI may impose a margin of 5% to 10% over non-government securities for the purpose of SLR, in order to absorb the market risk. This will make pricing of Treasury instruments more competitive. The change in composition of SLR assets will broaden the market.

(C) Restrictions Placed by the Regulatory Environment

Lastly, the market deficiencies also arise from certain restrictive regulatory practices which are not consistent with a healthy money market. There are two areas where the market growth is stunted owing to such practices.

Firstly, the Repurchase Agreement or Repo is a popular instrument of monetary control for central banks all over the world. The Repo also adds to market liquidity by facilitating secured short- term lending. There is no reason why Repos should be allowed only on Government Securities and public sector bonds. As on date RBI is the only counter-party for Repos and there is no corporate or interbank market in this area. For a long time, RBI has been only a borrower under Repos, and hence the Repo as a money market instrument has not been effective. Repo with RBI also is limited to a maximum of 14 days and are subscribed by the banks only when they are not able to lend in call market. In my view interbank Repo can be done for periods six months to one year as well.

There is also no level playing field for all the players in money market. Financial institutions can lend freely but borrow only on term basis and hence are not active participants in the money market. Mutual Funds can only lend and till recently could not participate in the Repos.

Only recently RBI has allowed Insurance Companies, Mutual Funds and Non-Bank Finance Companies to participate in the Repo market. However, unless RBI allows Repos on all instruments, Repo market may not improve significantly.

Financial Institutions while participating in the money market are not yet subject to CRR and SLR requirements, hence there is no level playing ground for the bank to take the institutional competition. Only recently RBI has come out with a reserve requirement for the institutions, which is lower than that of the banks. It is necessary to allow financial institutions to participate in interbank money market fully on the same terms as commercial basis, i.e. with the same reserve requirement so as to avoid further distortion of interest rates.

There is a fall out of financial deregulation in that the financial institutions are undergoing a sort of despecialisation and are expanding into short-term lending. Similar developments have been witnessed in European countries, where a universal bank concept has been adopted as per second banking directive of EEC (*Quote.*" The feasibility of an efficient banking system has proved to be hardly compatible with high degree of specialisation and strong investment of public sector in credit institution" from "Interest Rate Liberalisation and Money Market Development", IMF, 1995). The distinction between banks and financial institutions (where were originally development banks) therefore gets blurred and it is all the more reason that both are treated on identical terms in money market.

There are two other aspects which Reserve Bank of India can take care of to develop a term money market and activate secondary market for non-government securities.

The RBI can offer a liquidity window, offering two-way quotes every day at specified time (say after clearing hours), whereby a bank may deposit or borrow funds. RBI's open market operations would be more effective if they adjust the rate mechanism and directly deal with the market. The spread may be adjusted depending on the RBI's view of liquidity and lending as a last resort at the end of the day will make call money market less volatile. RBI should also accept government and corporate securities for overnight lending through a liquidity window subject to certain norms. This is possible once the centralised settlement system as suggested earlier comes into operation. The lending against securities may be on softer terms as compared to unsecured lending. RBI may also lay down exposure norms for each of the banks under both the types of overnight lending.

These changes would obviate the need for Repos and Refinance, which may be phased out in course of time.

The evolution of money market would further strengthen financial markets and would also help generate a hedging mechanism. Financial innovation occurs on account of volatility in the markets, and with improved access to technology. Innovation is classified by Bank for International Settlements into four categories as price-risk transferring innovation, credit risk transferring innovation, liquidity generating instruments and equity generating investments. Any innovation is primarily aimed at : (i) redistributing the risk, and (ii) creation of liquidity—the areas where banks specialise. Nevertheless, it is a challenging area for the banks who are traditionally used to deal with only credit risk.

I may now make a brief reference to RBI's monetary policy in the context of deregulation, since it bears heavily on development of money market. The progress of financial deregulation in India followed world-wide trend. Interest rate restrictions were removed rightly, after controlling the NPA level in commercial banks and when inflation has reached historically low levels. The deregulation is synchronised with entry of new private and foreign banks and part privatisation of public sector banks. The markets have thus become sufficiently competitive to take in their stride the effects of deregulation. High liquidity in the market has prevented a rate-war amongst banks for attracting new deposits. We are, however, facing the paradox where high liquidity in coexisting with low rate of inflation and despite historically low level of interest rates the real interest rates are significantly higher than the rates prevailing in global markets.

The RBI may welcome to low rate of inflation as price stability is an objective of monetary policy. However, I am apprehensive whether the low inflation is indicative of recession, particularly, as evidenced from inventory build up and lower profits in basic industries such as Steel, Cement and Fertilisers as also in part of the consumer sector such as automobiles and white good industries. What is tolerable level of inflation is a debatable point. The Chakravarty Committee Report (of 1985) states a rate of 4%, which I think should more likely be in the range of 6% to 8% in a developing economy like ours. Banks are concerned since a low rate of growth may mean low off-take of credit, which dampens the entire interest rate structure. RBI has already enhanced the liquidity in the markets by a gradual reduction of CRR (release of resources on account of cut in CRR since April, 1996, is around Rs. 20,000 crores) and a further liquidity overflow is expected in view of RBI's continuing efforts to stem the appreciation of Dollar.

Under the circumstances, it is for consideration whether price stability (i.e., low rate of inflation) should in fact be such a dominant objective, even if it were to amount to, decreased economic activity. It is indeed a tight rope work for the policy framers to achieve goals of lower inflation rate, adequate level of production, and viability of banking system at one go; but it is to be appreciated that the ultimate aim of financial reforms would be to oil the real sector, i.e. development of real sector is the real proof of effectiveness of financial reforms. The problems associated with inflation and growth and the trade-offs involved in managing the two are universal and not India specific.

The lower nominal interest rates have not been able to stimulate demand for credit, for various macro-economic reasons which are open to debate. When we look at monetary aggregates, it is causing concern that expansion of M3 is in the range of 15% to 20%, while growth rate remains around 5.5% p.a. A low growth rate with high liquidity is not an ideal mix for a developing economy. The tendency for central banks in developing countries is to shift to indirect instruments of monetary policy such as open market operations, as against direct intervention through reserve ratios and regulation of interest rates. The multiplier rate in Indian economy is traditionally low (3.5% to 4%) on account of high reserve ratios. The low multiplier ratio in effect, blunts the efficiency of open market operations of RBI. I am sure, that phased implementation of CAC recommendations for full convertibility would help the markets to become more integrated. An integrated market is the best check and the monetary policy would be more effective if the market-driven rates are accepted as sign-posts of future growth.

In conclusion, I would like to repeat some of my earlier suggestions, to achieve an efficiency of money market, which in turn would strengthen the whole structure of financial markets. The RBI should establish a Central Settlement Agency along with a screen-based anonymous trading system to create a nation-wide money market. RBI should lift the remaining restrictions on financial institutions to participate in money market and secondary market, and the FIs should be subject to the same discipline applicable to the banks with regard to reserve ratios. RBI should open a liquidity window with daily quotes, for clean as also secured inter-bank lending as well as borrowing. There is need for more eligible instruments for the purpose of SLR. Banks should take initiative in developing risk management products and progress of convertibility of Rupee is a help in this direction.

2

Functioning of Money Market in a Market Economy with Reference to India

DEV RAJ

INTRODUCTION

Money Market and Market Economy are associated with the process of economic development. It prescribes a strategy of relationship between the market economy and money market in the recent process of globalisation, liberalisation and their impact on the functioning of 'money market' in a market economy.

Analytically, money market is very much like markets for goods and services. As such, the money market has its own demand, supply, competition, quantities, prices, etc. Financial markets are mainly called money markets or capital markets. The former are markets which deals in short-term funds, while the latter deals in long-term funds. We have interpreted the term 'Money Market' more broadly to include within its folds also the national money market of monetary theory. This market is co-terminous with the entire economy. The asset it deals in is money: the demanders are the holders of money, i.e. the public and the suppliers are the Government, the Central Bank (RBI in India) and other banks.

Money itself is acquired in the normal process of selling goods, services, and assets in all markets, as money is the common medium of exchange in all monetised transactions. There is no special or separate market for money like the ones, we have for bills, bonds or equity shares.

By 'Money Market' we mean the market for money as explained above. But in business parlance, the term 'money market' is almost always used in the sense of short-term credit market.

Normally, the term 'market' refers to a certain locality or geographical area where the traders and buyers conduct business transactions. In a purely literal sense, the money market transacts, purchases and sells in money. The commodity traded on the money market is "liquidity". Since, liquidity is frequently of International dimensions, all those financial papers which compete with money for liquidity, i.e. near money, are traded in the money market.

Functional-*cum*-Institutional classification of financial markets can be given in Figure 1.

Money markets play an important role in the deployment of short-term funds, and in signalling trends in liquidity and interest rates. These markets, therefore, provide information for monetary policy formulation and management.

The recent reforms in the Secondary market focused concern on:

(i) Improving market transparency;
(ii) Integrity; and
(iii) Infrastructure.

The Figure 2 explains the Indian financial system and roles of players (see Figure 2).

Following are the pre-requisites in brief, which are required for the development of money market:

(i) Highly developed and organised Commercial Banking System;
(ii) Presence of Central Bank;
(iii) Availability of proper credit-instruments;

FIG. 1

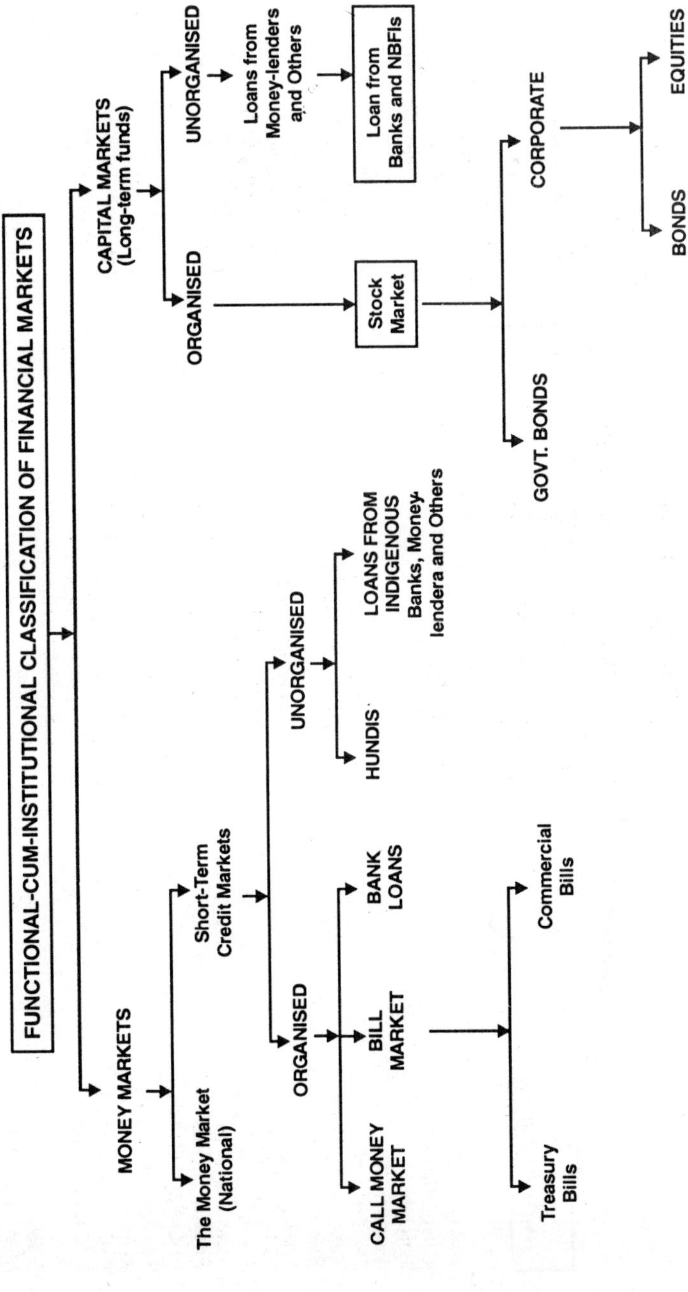
FUNCTIONAL-CUM-INSTITUTIONAL CLASSIFICATION OF FINANCIAL MARKETS
MONEY MARKETS
CAPITAL MARKETS (Long-term funds)
The Money Market (National)
Short-Term Credit Markets
ORGANISED
UNORGANISED
CALL MONEY MARKET
BILL MARKET
BANK LOANS
HUNDIS
LOANS FROM INDIGENOUS Banks, Money-lendera and Others
Treasury Bills
Commercial Bills
ORGANISED
UNORGANISED
Loans from Money-lenders and Others
Loan from Banks and NBFIs
Stock Market
GOVT. BONDS
CORPORATE
BONDS
EQUITIES

FIGURE 2

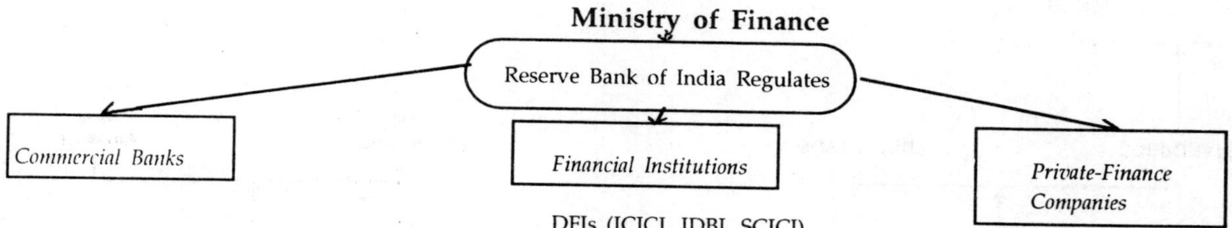

Commercial Banks	Financial Institutions	Private-Finance Companies
Private Government Foreign	DFIs (ICICI, IDBI, SCICI) Investment Institutions (UTI, LIC)	Housing Finance Cos. Hire Purchase Companies
Resource Base: Rs. 4,000 bn. Retail and Whole Sale deposits	*Resource Base:* Rs. 1,500-2,000 bn. Whole sale deposits	*Resource Base:* Rs. 400 bn. Retail deposits, bank/ FI Funding
Lending Activities: Working-Capital Lending Small-project loans Loans to Priority Sectors (e.g. Agriculture)	*Lending activities:* Large/medium-scale project loans Lease and equipment Finance.	*Lending activities:* Lease, hire-purchase Consumer loans, Truck/ Car Financing.
Fee Activities: Remittances Forex transactions L/Cs, guarantees.	*Fee Activities:* L/Cs, Project guarantees, Merchant Banking Advisory services. Custodial services.	*Fee Activities:* Merchant Banking Advisory services.
Subsidiaries: Merchant Banking Asset Management Housing Finance.	*Subsidiaries:* Asset Management Stock brokinig, money-market dealing, Commercial Banking	*Subsidiaries:* Asset Management Stock broking Money market operations

(iv) Existence of sub-markets;
(v) Availability of sufficient resources; and
(vi) Other factors.

FUNCTIONING OF CAPITAL MARKET

In contrast to the money market, which is the market for very short-term loans, the Capital Market is the market for medium-term and long-term loans. The money market, too, serves the needs of the discount market, whereas the capital market serves the need of industry and commerce, Governments and local authorities. Business firms often borrow their circulating capital from the commercial banks, but raise their fixed capital by issue or shares from their own reserves, the shares being taken up by individuals, insurance companies, investment trusts and unit trust. Limited companies also go to the Capital Market to borrow by means of debentures, the Government, or a local authority, by the issue of a new stock. Most stocks are redeemable at a specified future date—ten, fifty, or more years ahead.

Discount market is a market in which the principal business has to do with bills of exchange. The money market is the market for very short-term loans, and the discount market as the market is concerned with the discounting of bills of exchange—they are so intimately linked that the two terms are often regarded as synonymous. The members of these markets comprise the commercial banks, the agents of branches of some foreign banks, RBI/the Bank of England in case of United Kingdom in its capacity as "lender of last resort", the discount houses and the accepting houses or merchant banks. The 'Commodity' coming on to this market is the bill of exchange which at one time was not only the principal means of foreign trade payment but also widely used internationally.

Insofar as the capital market in India is concerned, I would like to stress that both the segments, viz. the primary market and secondary market are equally important while not being mutually exclusive. In fact, in my view, when a country's primary market is alive, it is possible to ensure a good degree of activity in the secondary market because it is the primary market which will ensure a continuous flow of securities to the secondary market, more so in developing economies.

Looking from the other angle, if a country's secondary

market is only active but not transparent and disciplined, the cult of equity and related investment in the primary market will be difficult to be continuously developed and sustained because the liquidity which the secondary market imparts to such investments in the hands of the investors will be adversely affected. Capital market has emerged as a major source of finance for the corporate sector. As far as the primary market is concerned the amount raised by the companies in the late seventies was around Rs. 90 crores a year. It increased to Rs. 22,000 crores in the year 1993-94, Rs. 10,369 crores during April-December, 1996, which was down from Rs. 14151 crores during April-Dec. 1995. Over the same months, the number of issues fell correspondingly from 1132 in 1995 to 793 in 1996, but the average size of the issue rose marginally from Rs. 12.50 crores to Rs. 13.07 crores.

The declining trend in issues and funds raised through the primary market is expected to continue in the short-run.

TABLE 1

Issues Launched

(Rs. in Crores)

Types of Issues	*1994-95*		*1995-96*		*1995 (April-December)*		*1996 (April-Dec.)*	
	No.	*Amount*	*No.*	*Amount*	*No.*	*Amount*	*No.*	*Amount*
Rights	324	6677	299	6564	209	4457	112	1750
Public	1342	21044	1426	14241	923	9694	681	8619
Total	1666	27621	1725	20805	1132	14151	793	10369

The market capitalisation has also grown rapidly, from Rs. 6750 crores in 1980 to over Rs. 3,40,000 crores in 1993-94, Rs. 4,86,192 crores in December, 1995 and Rs. 4,77,425 crores as on December, 1996. This period also witnessed a tremendous rise in the investor population from about 2 million to around 40 million, including those with the mutual funds. Money market is essentially a market for short-term, i.e. less than one year. The transactions in money market relates to : (i) Short-term Government debt-obligations, (ii) Bankers' acceptances; and (iii) Commercial papers. Thus, we can say that money market is for all the facilities of the country for the borrowing and lending of money for short-term.

The composition of Money Market can be explained as under:

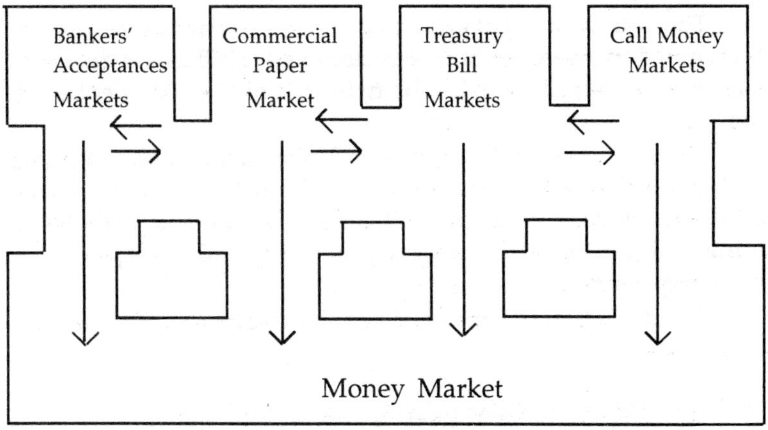

The above shows the very close relationship between different parts of money market and their relationship with the money market as a whole.

In the Secondary Market, the number of Stock Exchanges has gone upto 21 including the OTCEI while the NSE has become its proud addition. The number of listed companies has increased from about 2300 to around 7,500.

The daily turnover has also jumped from about Rs. 25 crores in 1979-80 to Rs. 800 crores in 1993-94. The core components of this reform programme are:

(a) Industrial Policy Reforms.
(b) Trade Policy and Exchange Control reforms.
(c) Financial Sector reforms.
(d) Public Enterprises reforms.
(e) Increased direct foreign investment.

It should also be acknowledged that the structure of the market has evidenced significant change and development, with the establishment over the years of merchant banking and financial services comparisons, more stock exchanges, mutual funds, venture capital funds, credit rating agencies, portfolio management services, registrars to issues, stock depository and custodial service agencies, etc. The emphasis now is on to improve the levels of disclosures and to see that financial accounting statements move towards international standards.

The role of a regulatory body in the securities market is determined by the stage of its development. SEBI as a regulatory body has necessarily to play the twin role of 'development' and 'regulation'.

The regulation of the capital market should aim at protecting the investor interest against possible risks and fraud. As regards the money market, as mentioned earlier the last few years have witnessed efforts at broadening activity and creation of a secondary market.

The definition of Primary Capital is composed of following elements:—

(i) Partly or fully paid-up share capital,
(ii) Share premimum,
(iii) General Reserves,
(iv) The balance on the Profit and Loss Accounts,
(v) Minority interests in consolidated subsidiaries.
(vi) General Bad Debt Provisions, less any associated deferred tax asset, and (vii) Allowable Perpetual debt. In other words, we can say that capital elements are—

Tier 1

(a) Ordinary Paid-up Share Capital/Common stock.
(b) Disclosed Reserves.

Tier 2

(a) Undisclosed resources.
(b) Asset Revaluation resources,
(c) General Provisions/general loan loss reserves,
(d) Hybrid (debt/equity) capital instruments, and
(e) Subordinated Term Debt.

To a large extent, banks turn to call money market whenever they are short of funds to maintain the statutory minimum balances with the RBI. Section 42(1) of RBI Act stipulates that banks should maintain a prescribed portion of their net demand and time liablities at the end of a fortnight as statutory balances to be maintained with the RBI (CRR balances) during the subsequent fortnight. Call money market is an integral part of the Indian money market, where day to day surplus funds are normally traded for short durations ranging from one day to 14 days or more.

The Report of the Committee to Review the Working of the Monetary System," (Chakravarty Committee) 1985, recommended that a "Working Group may be formed to study the operations of money market and to suggest remedial measures.

MARKET EFFICIENCY OF CAPITAL FOR AN MARKET ECONOMY

The Kaldor's (1982) representation of supply and demand for money is quite relevant for Market Economy. The same can be explained as under:

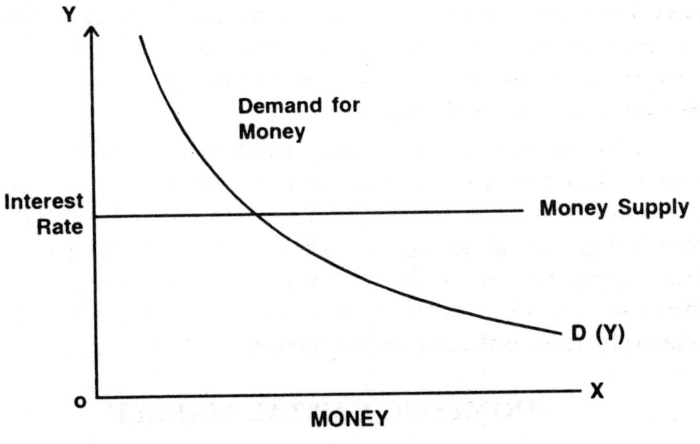

The Working Group appointed by RBI under the Chairmanship of N. Vaghul, the then Chairman of ICICI, recommended (1987) for widening and deepening of the call money market by selective increase in the number of participants and by injecting new instruments.

It also recommended for withdrawing the ceiling limit, so that the Call Money rate could be determined solely by the market forces of demand and supply. In pursuance of the recommendations, the RBI initiated a number of measures such as:

(a) setting up of DFHI in March, 1988 to create a secondary market for new instruments and in July, 1988 permitting DFHI to participate in the Call Money market both as a borrower and as a lender; and
(b) increasing the number of participants in the market by permitting GIC, IDBI, and NABARD as lenders in April, 1990.

The ceiling on call money rate was withdrawn with effect from Ist May, 1989. Since, then, the rate was determined by market forces. It was evident that the fortnightly variations were influenced not only by pure market mechanisms but also to a marked degree by the cash reserve ratio (CRR) requirements of the banks. After the removal of the ceiling on call money rate the call money market went through a period of high volatility. The call market which is frequently accessed by the commercial banks to borrow funds for fulfulling their statutory obligation in respect of CRR, went through a major upheavel during the year 1991 and 1992.

Fluctuations in call money market are neither new nor unexpected. Interest rate fluctuations in call money markets is a national phenomenon in any financial system. Essentially, the rate changes in call money markets are influenced by the demand and supply for/or funds mainly from the banking sector and the flow of funds into the market from the banks, FIs and other relatively new entrants to the system.

DOMESTIC CAPITAL MARKET

In the Capital Market the suppliers of funds, Intermediaries and Demanders of funds can be summarised as on next page.

The creation of domestic capital market includes the following principle measures:

(1) Freeing interest rates;
(2) Eliminating or dramatically reducing existing

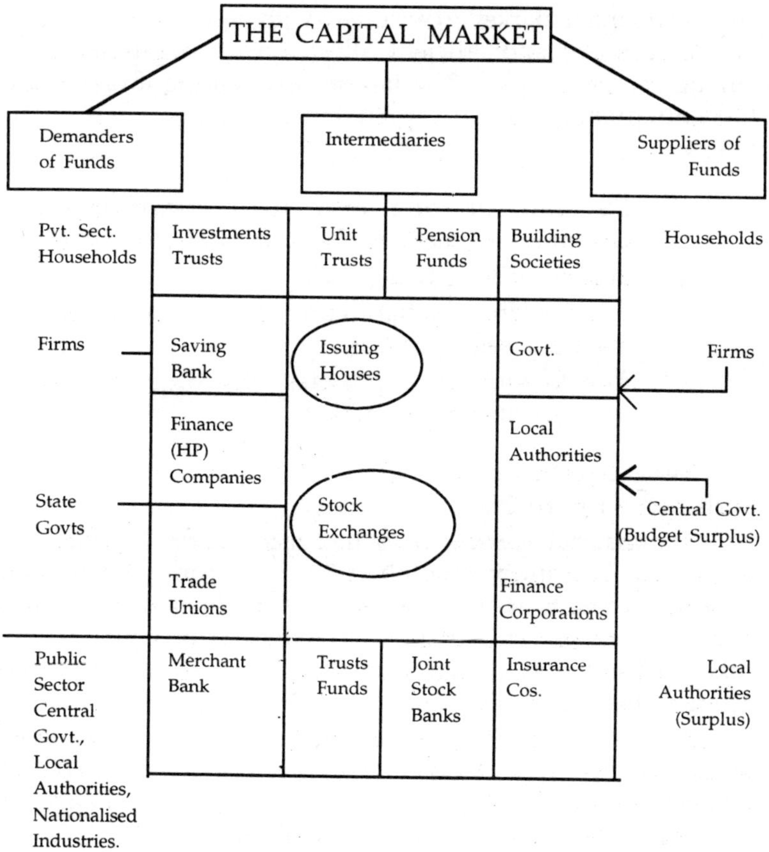

qualitative and quantitative controls over credit (e.g. by sector of activity, type of collateral size of firm, use of credit);

(3) Reducing the barriers to entry for new banks, financial intermediaries, and foreign banks (especially in Argentina and Chile);

(4) The progressive reduction of reserve requirements; and

(5) The return or auction to the private sector of the bulk of the banks, which has been placed under state control.

The capital market is concerned with promotion of Savings and Investment and efficient allocation of long-term funds among competing uses. The liasion between the investor and the entrepreneur in the capital market can be summed as follow:

(i) Demand for long-term funds constitutes one important segment in the structural framework;
(ii) Supply of long-term funds;
(iii) Financial Intermediaries providing linkage constitute the third segment;
(iv) The Government policies affecting the above components of the market.

Structured framework of Capital Market in India may be explained on page 29.

For financial opening up to the outside world the following steps are to be implemented liberally: (i) Authorisation to open banking accounts within the country dominated in foreign currency; and (ii) The progressive reduction of limits on the entry and out flow of capital, both as well as limits on the accounts that could flow in.

In short, much as liberalisation stimulated financial intermediation, the Capital Market remained largely segmented and underdeveloped, especially as far as long-term credit is concerned. The same can be put as under:

$$M + C = Pk + Pd\ D + F$$

Where: M=Wealth, C=Credit, K=Capital goods, D=Durable goods Pk and Pd = Prices of Capital of Consumer-durable goods; and F = Financial assets.

The flow of goods and resources in an economic system can be explained on page 30.

Volatility of Capital Markets, exchange rate fluctuations, uncertainties in resource flows, uncertainties in the cost of borrowing, fluctuations in the terms of trade, are some of the examples in this regards.

These volatilities have significant destability effect on the process of development in the developing countries, in

Structural Framework of Capital Market in India

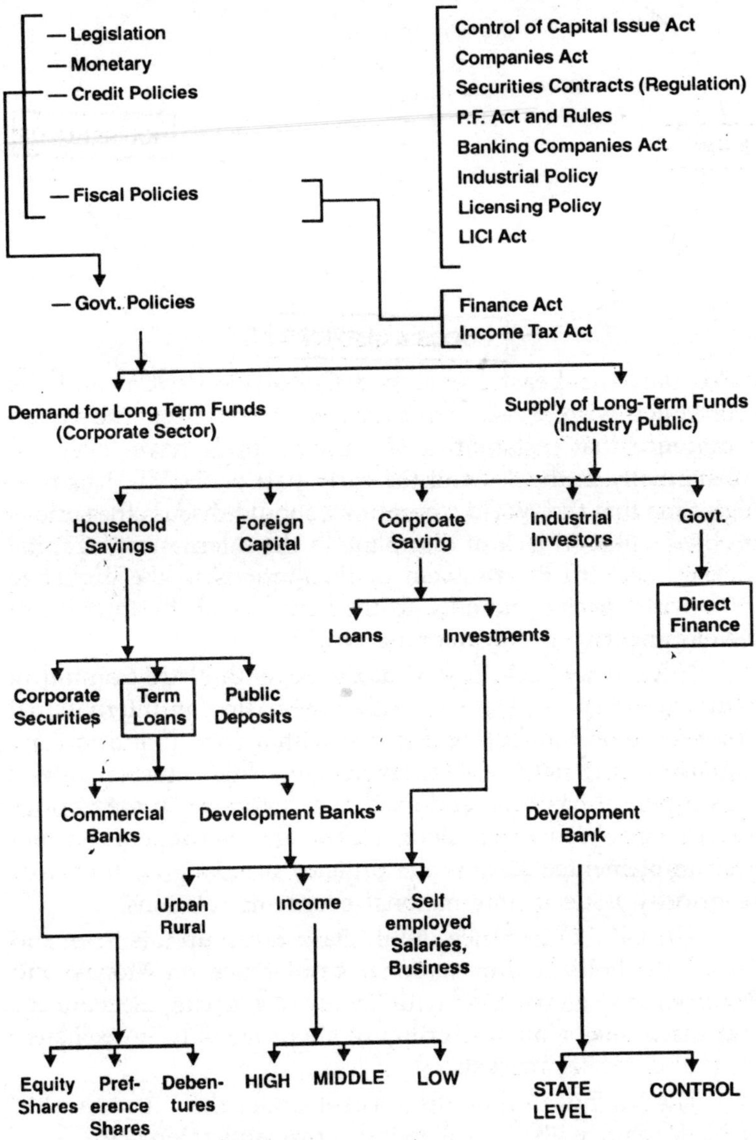

*[IFCI, ICICI, CDCS, NIDC, IDBI, IRBI]

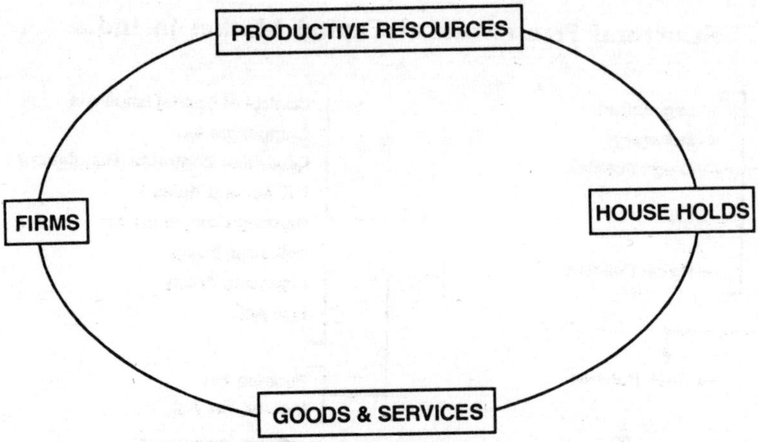

particular, the Least Developed Countries (LDCs) and the economies with weak governments. It has been the recent experience that instabilities of various funds have increased substantially in the 80s and the early part of the 90s. It is now high time that the World community should discuss the serious problems like: (i) lack of discipline in the international Capital Market; and (ii) the problem of fluctuations in the exchange rates with special reference to their impact on the process of development in the developing world.

It was way back in 1983 at the Seventh NAM Summit in New Delhi that a plea was made for holding an International Conference on Money and Finance with a view to introducing stability in the field of "exchange rates" and "interest rates". This proposal has been endorsed and reiterated in the various fora in the subsequent periods. However, this proposal has not been implemented despite the urgency of taking up this issue as priority issue in international economic relations.

The G-77 Conference should have taken up this issue and resolve to hold an International Conference on Money and Finance at the global level with a view to evolving mechanisms and disciplines aimed at bringing about stability in exchange rates and capital markets.

The Vaghul Committee was set under the Chairmanship of N. Vaghul with the following terms and reference:

— To examine Money market instruments and recommend specific measures for their development.

— To recommend the pattern of money market interest rates and to indicate whether these should be administered or determined by the Market.
— To study the feasibility of increasing the participation in the Money Market.
— To assess the impact of changes in the cash credit system on the money market and to examine the need for developing specialised institutions such as discount houses. In this context, the inter-action between the inter-corporate market and expanded money market could also be examined.
— Any other issue having a bearing on the development of the money market.

The Vaghul Committee in its Report (5th September, 1986) made the following suggestions for the improvement of Capital Market in India:

— Lowering of the Discount Rate applicable to Bill from the ceiling of 16.75% to 15.5%,
— Government directives to be issued to all public sector undertakings that payments for all Credit Purchases made by them should be made in the form of Bills,
— Penalty for not honouring the Bills on due date,
— Specific stipulation by RBI directing a phased increase in the proportion of bill acceptance to total credit purchases to a level of 75% by April, 1987.
— Establishment of a Finance House to ensure emergence of an active secondary market for bills, besides simplification in the procedure for bills rediscounting.

The Vaghul Committee recommended the following:

(1) To improve the Call Money market.
(2) To improve the Bills Rediscounting.
(3) Short-term Commercial Paper.
(4) Government Paper.
(5) Setting up of a Finance House
(6) Development of New Instruments.

(7) Inter-Bank Participation Certificates.
(8) Certificates of Deposit.
(9) Factoring services.
(10) Legislative changes.

DEVELOPMENT OF MONEY MARKET IN A MARKET ECONOMY

From Annexure I, a brief position of International Bond Issues issued by developing countries during the years 1993 to 1996 may be seen. The amount under the International Bond issued by all the developing countries increased from US $ 47104 million in 1993 to US $ 81669 million in the year 1996.

Out of this, 57.47% share is of Latin-American and the Caribean countries with an amount of issue of US $ 46932 million in 1996. The Europe and Central Asian countries canvassed the amount of US $ 11534 million in 1996 and are having a percentage share of 14.12% in all the developing countries. The East Asian and the Pacific countries canvassed the amount under bond to the tune of US $ 19629 million and secured 2nd position by having a share of 24.03% during the year 1996.

While the amount canvassed under International Equity Issues by developing countries increased from US $ 10980 million in 1993 to US $ 18482 million in 1994, came down to US $ 8730 million in 1995 and then again increased to US $ 11754 million in 1996. During the year 1996, the East Asia and the Pacific countries achieved the Ist position by having Equity Issues amounting to US $ 4077 million with 34.68% share during the year 1996. The second position was achieved by Latin American and Caribbean countries by having Equity Issues amounting to US$ 3661 million with a share of 31.5% among all the developing countries. The other details may be seen from the Annexure-II, i.e. International Equity Issues by developing countries during the years 1993 to 1996.

Annexure III gives in detail the month-wise Implict yield of 91-day-T-Bills at cut of Price for the years 1993-94 to 1996-97. While Annexure IV gives the details of Net Market Borrowings of Central Government for the years 1992-93 to 1995-96 and 1996-97.

In the Indian stock market the following drawbacks have been observed:

(i) Lack of control over the fair disclosure of financial information;
(ii) Non-development of secondary market;
(iii) Passive role of public financial institutions in checking the malpractices;
(iv) Manipulation of security prices;
(v) Insider trading;
(vi) Unofficial trade in the primary market; and
(vii) Existence of improper control over brokers and sub-brokers.

The Government of India has adopted policies of globilisation, liberalisation and market economy in the wake of the serious economic crisis that enveloped the country by the middle of 1991.

The crisis arose due to the economic consequences of upheavals in the erstwhile USSR and East Europe—the effects of the Gulf War, the shifts in the global economic power balance and the economic policies followed by the Union and the State Governments. India's adoption of a programme of globilisation, market economy and competiveness came after more than six months of negotiations with the World Bank starting in January, 1991. The package of reform measures announced in July, 1991 consisted of two separate economic policies:

(a) a macro-economic stabilisation programme (IMF inspired) essentially focusing on reducing the twin deficits on Balance of Payment and on the State budget; and
(b) a comprehensive programme for structural change of the economy (World Bank inspired) in the fields of trade, industry, foreign investments, public sector and the financial sector among others.

"Globilisation", "Competition" and "Liberalisation" came to India as a booster, and through the backdoor of "Economic reforms"..

It was argued that progress is taking place through globilisation and economic reforms are the only means to join in this process. Hence, economic reforms are the only alternative for human security and India's future.

Globilisation as a phenomenon involves access to two different entities:

(a) Finance capital through MNCs; and
(b) new technologies, such as computers and telecommunications.

Some economists in India have recommended a synthesised paradigm of "Socially Responsible Market Economy" (SRME), which needs to be evolved and given a concrete shape before it can be operationalised and implemented.

The economic basis of the SRME paradigm lies in taking the market economy close to the concept of a perfectly competitive market economy. The ultimate goal of SRME is maximisation of people's welfare, reconciling and satisfying interests of all economic players, including consumers, producers, distributors and earners (from land, capital and enterprise). RBI Governor C. Rangarajan has constituted a Standing Committee on money market under the Chairmanship of Y.V. Reddy, Deputy Governor, RBI.

The Committee will analyse the following areas in detail:

(i) to advise on the measures needed to ensure orderly functioning of the call money market including the payment and settlement systems, implications of reserve requirements of the banking system, money supply and term in money market;
(ii) to strengthen the role of call money market in the financial system;
(iii) to suggest measures for developing secondary market for money market instruments;
(iv) to assess and advise on evolving desirable linkages between the money market, foreign exchange, Government securities and capital markets;
(v) to tender advice on any other specific issue referred to it by the RBI and will examine other issues having a bearing on the development of money market.

It may be recalled that in the monetary and credit policy for the first half of 1997-98 announced on April, 15, 1997 the RBI has hinted that a Committee would be formed to advise the RBI for developing the money market further and making it more efficient, by planning to improve in the following areas:

(a) reinstating the importance of the bank rate, virtually linking every rate to it;
(b) greater operational freedom to banks relaxing several direct controls;
(c) Plans to strengthen the money market; and
(d) measures to increase the resource flows to agriculture sector, etc.

For money market lending through any primary dealer, the minimum transaction size has been reduced from Rs. 20 crores to Rs. 10 crores. All gilts are made eligible for repo transactions; non-bank SGL account holders have been permitted to put through reverse repo-transactions.

Treasury bills of varying maturities are to be introduced. ADs have been allowed to effect cross border money market operations.

Strange as it may sound, there is a glimmer of hope in the pall of gloom surrounding the primary market. The response to public issues from investments during 1996-97 was dismal. The truth is that the market today is a far cry from what it was some years ago. Gone are the days when any promoter could come to the market and raise money from a gullible public—only to disappear a few month later. During the year 1996-97, a sum of only Rs. 2734 crores was raised through rights issues as against Rs. 6520 crores raised during the year 1995-96, which reflects that these days the market has matured enough.

FUTURE OF MONEY MARKET IN A MONEY ECONOMY

The process of Capital Market reforms was carried forward during 1996-97 and 1997-98 with an array of reforms encompassing primary and secondary markets for equity and debt, and foreign institutional investment.

Primary market reforms aimed at providing greater flexibility to the issuers and strengthening the criteria for securities market. Reforms in the secondary market focused on improving market transparency, integrity and infrastructure. The first depository was launched in Oct. 1996. This will help to ease the bottlenecks associated with a higher volume of paper work and boost the process of dematerilisation of scripts.

A modified take over code and a stock lending scheme have been approved by SEBI. Despite the maintenance of the pace of capital market reforms, market developments presented a different picture.

The primary market was characterised by a reduced number of issues and lower amounts raised, while the secondary market witnessed low trading volumes and declining of generally subdued market sentiment. Most mutual fund schemes attracted lukewarm response from the investors. However, the securities markets attracted foreign institutional investment at almost double the level of the previous year.

The Government securities market swa a strengthening of primary dealer system. The excess demand for investment funds moderated and the liquidity conditions eased in early 1996-97. The yield to maturity on auctioned -91-day treasury bills fell steadily to 6.92% in November, 1996 from the high of 12.97% at the beginning of the year. The fall in the yield of 364 day treasury bills was relatively less pronounced, but it also fell to 10.33% by end December, 1996 from 13.12% in end-March, 1996. The coupon rate on 10 year GOI bonds fell only marginally to 13.85% in 1996-97 from 14% in 1995-96.

This significant softening in the cut-off yields along with the decline in the call rates indicated an easing of demand-supply gaps in the money and credit market conditions. For the success of monetary and credit policy, the character of the money market is important. The unorganised sector of the market is practically insulated from monetary and credit controls. The RBI has no control over the quantity and composition of credit in this market. This works as an important limitation to the working of monetary policy in India. But since, 1947, the situation is rapidly changing with the fast expansion of banking in the country and the relative shrinkage of the unoragnised sector of the money market

The economic function of future markets depends upon the various factors like: clearing houses, margin money, the spreads among future prices, the importance of spreads to future markets, the behaviour of spreads, etc. The competition in the international market economy reveals the following realities of the market:

(i) Discloses knowledge;
(ii) Enhances efficiency; and
(iii) Restrains Power.

In short, the Indian money market has remained divided into two more or less water-tight compartments and still is deficient in the areas of proper control over the fair disclosure of financial information, inadequate secondary market, passive role of public financial institutions in checking the malpractices, manipulation of security prices, inside trading, unofficial trade in the primary market, inadequate control over brokers and sub-brokers, etc. The future of market depends upon the various contributory factors such as clearing houses, margin money, the spreads among future prices, the importance of spreads to future markets and the behaviour of spreads.

ANNEXURE I

International Bond Issues by Developing Countries During 1993 to 1996

(Million US $)

S. No.	*Region/Group of Countries*	*1993*	*1994*	*1995*	*1996*
1	2	*3*	*4*	*5*	*6*
1.	Sub-Saharan Africa	0.00	1317	1242	1220
		(0.00)	(3.22)	(2.73)	(1.49)
2.	East Asia & the Pacific	7714	13028	10156	19629
		(16.38)	(31.87)	(22.34)	(24.03)
3.	South Asia	556	1078	782	1357
		(1.18)	*(2.64)*	*(1.72)*	*(1.66)*
	Of which:—				
	India	556	883	770	1107
4.	Europe & Central Asia	13605	7218	9410	11534
		(28.88)	(17.66)	(20.70)	(14.12)
5.	Latin American & the Caribbean	25231	17555	22827	16932
		(53.56)	(42.95)	(50.22)	(57.41)
6.	Middle East & North Africa	0.00	678	1038	998
		(0.00)	(1.66)	(2.28)	(1.22)
All Developing Countries		47104	40874	45456	81669
		(100.00)	(100.00)	(100.00)	(100.00)

Source: Global Development Finance: Volume I—Analysis Summary Tables 1997, A World Bank Book.

ANNEXURE II

International Equity Issues by Developing Countries 1993 to 1996

(Million US $)

S. No.	*Region/Country*	*1993*	*1994*	*1995*	*1996*
1	*2*	*3*	*4*	*5*	*6*
1.	Sub-Sharan Africa	126 (1.15)	638 (3.45)	393 (4.50)	761 (6.47)
2.	East Asia and the Pacific	2635 (24.00)	6818 (36.89)	6317 (72.36)	4077 (34.68)
3.	*South Asia*	340 (3.10)	4271 (23.11)	281 (3.22)	1340 (11.40)
	Of which: India	340	3029	274	1340
4.	Europe and Central Asia	191 (1.74)	717 (3.88)	860 (9.85)	1506 (12.81)
5.	Latin America and Caribbean:	7688 (70.02)	6037 (32.66)	845 (9.68)	3661 (31.15)
6.	Middle East and North Africa	0 (0.00)	0 (0.00)	34 (0.39)	410 (3.49)
All Developing Countries		10980 (100.00)	18482 (100.00)	8730 (100.00)	11754 (100.00)

Note: Figures in brackets are the percentage share to total during the year.
Source: Global Development Finance, Volume I—Analysis and Summary Tables-1997: A World Bank Book.

ANNEXURE III

Implicit Yield of 91 Day-T-Bills at Cut of Price

(Per cent per annum)

Month	*1993-94*	*1994-95*	*1995-96*	*1996-97*
1	*2*	*3*	*4*	*5*
April	11.10	7.45	11.99	12.97
	10.76	7.33	11.99	12.84
	9.50	7.25	12.03	12.63
	9.50	7.25	11.90	12.46
	9.84	7.25	11.40	
May	9.75	7.21	11.95	12.41
	9.63	7.50	12.07	12.37
	9.71	7.58	12.07	12.37
	9.75	7.75	12.07	12.37
June	9.92	7.75	12.33	12.41
	9.96	8.00	12.33	12.41
	10.05	8.46	12.37	12.41
	10.09	8.75	12.58	12.41
July	10.05	9.08	12.71	12.41
	10.00	9.08	12.97	11.86
	9.84	8.91	12.97	9.88
	9.75	8.75	12.75	9.21
August	9.26	8.25	12.67	9.46
	9.33	8.00	12.67	9.04
	9.25	8.00	12.63	8.46
	9.17	8.08	12.58	9.46
September	9.08	8.08	12.54	9.96
	8.91	8.08	12.54	10.00
	8.71	8.41	12.54	10.13
	8.37	9.08	12.67	10.17

(Contd.)

1	2	3	4	5
October	8.37	9.21	12.67	10.17
	8.16	9.21	12.75	10.09
	8.08	8.50	12.80	10.05
	8.16	8.33	12.88	8.83
November	8.25	8.29	12.97	6.92
	8.16	8.25	12.97	7.21
	8.50	8.58	12.97	7.21
	8.62	8.75	12.97	8.16
December	8.58	9.00	12.97	8.04
	8.04	9.37	12.97	8.16
	7.96	9.75	12.97	8.16
	7.83	9.84	12.97	8.16
	7.79	10.26		
January	8.08	10.51	12.97	8.16
	8.32	10.85	12.97	8.16
	8.58	10.93	12.97	8.12
	8.50	11.10	12.97	8.00
			12.97	7.50
February	8.46	11.10	12.97	
	8.37	11.23	12.97	
	8.37	11.40	12.97	
	8.25	12.97	12.97	
			12.97	
March	7.83			12.97
	7.46			12.97
	7.08			12.97
	7.33			12.97
				12.97

Source: Various Issues of Economic Survey of India and Annual Report of the Reserve Bank of India.

ANNEXURE IV

Net Market Borrowings of the Central Government of India*

(Rs. Crores)

Instruments	*(April-March)*			*(April-December)*			
	1992-93	*1993-94*	*1995-96*	*1993-94*	*1994-95*	*1995-96*	*1996-97*
1. Conventional Market Borrowing	3670	3700	3700	3972	3700	3700	3025
2. Other Medium & Long-Term Borrowing	NIL	23842	29379	10992	13597	19879	15965
3. 364 days Treasury Bills	4791	–391	–6288	4070	3189	–6399	4783
Total	8641	27151	26790	19034	20486	17180	23773

*Actuals as per RBI records.

Source: Various issues of Economic Survey and the Reserve Bank of India Annual Reports.

ANNEXURE V
Stock Market Indicators

Indicator		*Index 1*		*Price/Earv. Ratio*		*Average Daily Turn-over (BSE) (Rs. Crores)*	*Market Capitalisation (Rs. Crores)*
		Senex	*Natex*	*Senex*	*Natex*		
1		*2*	*3*	*4*	*5*	*6*	*7*
1993:	April	2205.37	993.63	27.19	24.96	173	175093
	Dec.	3301.85	1589.25	40.02	40.28	438	305000
1994:	April	3824.75	1855.81	46.43	46.46	196	364868
	Dec.	3949.78	1876.13	34.50	38.58	423	400000
1995:	April	3359.27	1631.55	27.84	31.84	127	494908
	May	3206.09	1539.44	29.78	32.65	112	495414
	June	3336.46	1570 48	18.03	21.11	194	506780
	July	3334.86	1550.57	19.32	21.54	242	505592
	August	3402.81	1568.33	18.41	20.21	244	547424
	Sept.	3396.37	1555.07	18.67	20.15	239	576977
	Oct.	3528.10	1603.84	17.83	18.61	267	563721
	Nov.	3172.02	1442.54	15.44	16.71	183	472942
	Dec.	3060.05	1406.95	15.99	16.95	239	486192

1996 :							
	April	3599.66	1649.60	19.57	20.14	371	636868
	May	3732.20	1701.17	19.25	19.85	436	563739
	June	3906.72	1771.88	19.56	20.29	602	576973
	July	3668.21	1676.60	16.86	17.69	646	545150
	August	3449.17	1575.49	14.34	15.80	380	540340
	September	3390.11	1522.17	13.19	14.17	347	518266
	October	3154.38	1407.96	12.50	12.11	422	495440
	November	3052.83	1360.42	11.34	11.03	347	452989
	December	2918.68	1290.21	12.20	11.78	386	477425

Notes : 1. Average for the month Senex (base 1978-79=100) Natex (Base 1983-91=100).
2. Eatimated for all India.

Source: Compiled from the various issues of Economic Survey.

3

Evolution of Money Markets in India

Deepak Mohanty and Argya Kusum Mitra

The advanced market economies have well developed money markets. In developing countries the money market usually centres around the inter-bank call money market. However, in their effort to move away from direct instruments of monetary control to indirect instruments, governments and central banks in many developing countries have made special efforts to develop their money markets. In India, the inter-bank call money market formed the core of money market till the late 1980s. The Committee to review the working of the monetary system (Chakravarty Committee, 1985) underscored the need to enlarge the scope of money market which led to setting up of a Working Group (Vaghul Working Group, 1987) to recommend specific measures for evolving money market instruments in India. This paper attempts to briefly trace the evolution of money market in India. The paper has been organised as follows: Section I highlights the role of money market. Section II focuses on money market instruments and institutions in India. Section III attempts to capture relevant trends in money markets and offers the conclusions of the paper.

I

ROLE OF MONEY MARKET

The term 'Money Market' constitutes network of borrowers and lenders for short-term funds and includes all financial instruments which can be easily converted to means of payment (say, cash) without significant loss of value. The money market performs a crucial role in equilibrating short-term demand and supply of funds thereby facilitating the conduct of monetary policy. Generally, the short term is defined to include instruments with maturities up to one year. The major functions of the money market are:

- it enables liquidity management of participants;
- money market interest rates serve as reference rates for pricing debt instruments;
- government/central bank instruments are used as tools of monetary policy;
- it enables transformation of maturity.

While inter-bank money markets and central bank lending or discounting provide liquidity for banks, private non-bank money market instruments, such as commercial bills and commercial paper, provide liquidity to the commercial sector. The private instruments are particularly important in those countries where the rates are relatively free. The monetary authority uses money markets to adjust primary liquidity in the domestic economy through open market operations. Discounting of notes issued by the private sector and purchases of foreign exchange swap contracts are other ways of adjusting liquidity used by emerging economies of Asia. For the money market rates to emerge as reference rate, it essential that the rates are market determined which then would achieve allocative efficiency. Otherwise, the pricing of debt instruments and chanelling of funds from savers to investors may not be optimised. Furthermore, the reference rate need not be a domestic one. The cross-country evidence shows that for small open economies without foreign exchange controls, the reference rate was external during the 1980s like the LIBOR plus a swap premium representing forex risk (Indonesia) and Singapore inter-bank offering rate for the US dollar or SIBOR (Hong Kong). By the end of 1980s, the money markets in most of the emerging economies of South-east Asia provided reference rates to their financial systems (e.g. SIBOR for Singapore and inter-bank rate for Malaysia). However, reference rates did not emerge in Korea and Philippines owing to the interference by monetary authorities (*Oularis,* 1995).

Players and Instruments in Money Market

Central banks provide advance and rediscounting facilities to ensure adequate liquidity in the short-term financial markets. They either lend directly to banks or indirectly through special intermediaries such as discount houses in London or primary dealers (PDs) in the US. The borrowers in the money market, in general, are the central and local governments, banks, FIs and corporates, while the lenders are the financial institutions (FIs), corporates, banks and financial intermediaries and households. Households, however, play a limited role in the money market, which is characterised by short-term, high volume flow of funds, thereby precluding individual participation. Individuals can participate in short-term financial market, through money market mutual funds (MMMFs), but such funds are not too common in most countries. The money market instruments consist of (i) deposits–call, time (of maturity less than one year), currency, certificates of deposit, (ii) treasury bills, (iii) other short-term government securities, (iv) bankers' acceptances/commercial bills, (v) commercial paper, (vi) MMMFs and (vii) inter-corporate funds.

Patterns of Money Market Development

After a cross-country examination of East Asian economies, Cole, Scott and Wellons (1995) observed that the money markets went through four similar stages of development during the 1980s: controlled system, initial liberalisation, retrenchment following a crisis and a more aggressive development. The first stage was characterised by barriers to entry and administered rates. The second step was to relax these controls which most emerging Asian countries did during the early 1980s. The third stage was to go one step backward following crises involving large changes in financial prices–either depreciation of the exchange rates or increases in interest rates that the government could not accept–entailing a curtailing of the money markets or the conduit through which price adjustments were happening. The fourth stage involved going two steps forward with governments adopting more aggressive policies to further free and develop the money market once the crisis was over. Money markets are still in the process of evolutionn in these economies.

II. THE INDIAN MONEY MARKET

The Indian money market was characterised by a limited number of participants, strict regulation of entry and a limited number of instruments till the late 1980s. The instruments were limited to call (overnight) and short-notice (up to fourteen days) money, inter-bank deposits/loans and bills rediscounting; although interest rates on money market instruments were tightly regulated, those were often breached, particularly during periods of tight liquidity.

Call Money

The call money market is a major segment of the money market. Till 1987, the participation in the call money market was limited to banks and two FIs-LIC and UTI; the entry of new players was strictly regulated. In December 1973, the hitherto free call money rates were subjected to a ceiling which was often breached. Recognising these weaknesses of the call money market, both the Chakravarty Committee (1985) and the Vaghul Working Group (1987) recommended freeing of call rates so that it could provide 'an equilibrating mechanism for evening out short-term surpluses and deficits' and provide the monetary authority 'a focal point' to 'intervene for influencing liquidity in the economy'. Accordingly, call rates were freed from the ceiling of 10 per cent, effective May 1, 1989. Furthermore, the Discount and Finance House of India (DFHI) started its operations in April 1988 in order to provide 'reasonable access to users of short-term money'.

During the 1990s, further liberalisation was effected:

- lending in the call market through the DFHI was made broad based;
- all participants in bills rediscounting market were allowed entry as lenders, effective October 1990;
- entry of new participants in the form of mutual funds–both in the public and the private sector–as lenders, and five more PDs as both borrowers and lenders;
- freeing of inter-bank liabilities from reserve requirements which would help generate a smooth yield curve and reduce volatility in the call rates which hitherto have depicted a cyclical pattern with troughs on reporting Fridays.

Commercial Bills Market

The commercial bill market, though an important segment in industrial countries, did not prove to be that successful in India due to the cash credit system of credit delivery where the onus of cash management rested with banks. Absence of an active secondary market further dampened the market for bills finance. The Chakravarty Committee was of the view that an active bill market would relieve the pressure on banks while providing banks with a financial instrument of acceptable liquidity, safety and return. The Vaghul Working Group had recommended the following measures to activate the moribund bills market:

- maximum discount rate should be lower than maximum lending rate;
- discontinuance of the ceiling on rediscount rate with development of the call money market;
- simplification of procedures for bills rediscounting;
- increased participation in the market.

Accordingly, the interest rate ceiling of 12.5 per cent on rediscounting of commercial bills, along with the interest rates ceiling on 10.5-11.5 per cent on inter-bank term money and 12.5 per cent on inter-bank participation were withdrawn, effective May 1, 1989. The success of the bills discounting scheme is contingent upon financial discipline on the part of borrowers. In the absene of such restraints, the Reserve Bank in July 1992 restricted the banks to finance bills to the extent of working capital needs based on credit norms. However, in order to encourage 'bills' culture, the Reserve Bank advised banks in October 1997 that at least 25 per cent of inland credit purchases of borrowers should be through bills.

Commercial Paper

Commercial paper consists of unsecured promissory notes sold either directly by the issuers to investors or through agents like merchant banks and security houses. In India, however, CPs are privately placed with investors through banks or FIs. This instrument facilitates highly rated corporates to raise short-term finance at relatively lower costs to meet their working capital requirements; often at rates lower than the PLR of banks. In India, therefore, the rise and fall in the outstanding amount of CPs is a fair indicator of the liquidity scenario of the economy. The Vaghul Working Group had recommended that:

- The discount rate to be market determined;
- Banks will reduce the permissible working capital limits to the extent of the amount of the issue of CP;
- Credit rating agencies to be a prerequisite for the development of the CP market.

Consequent to the implementation of the recommendations, CP was introduced in India in January 1990. Originally, intended only for top-rated clients, with a maturity of 91 days to 6 months at a freely determined discount to face value and a minimum size of Rs. 1 crore, the working capital credit limit of companies for issue of CP as well as minimum credit rating requirement have been progressively relaxed; while the minimum size stands reduced to Rs. 25 lakh, the maturity period is modified to 30 days-1 year. Although the withdrawal of stand-by facility in October 1994 and the introduction of the loan system for credit delivery in April 1995 adversely impacted, temporarily, on CP issues, the delinking of CP from the cash credit component of MPBF in October 1996 and easy liquidity conditions have imparted a renewed thrust to the CP market in recent months. Effective September 6, 1996 PDs were also permitted to issue CPs to access short-term funds.

Certificates of Deposit

A Certificate of Deposit (CD) is a document of title to a time deposit. It facilitates banks to raise bulk deposits at a lower transaction cost. Acknowledging imperfections in the money market, the Vaghul Working Group did not recommend the introduction of CDs; subsequently, however, CDs were introduced in June 1989. Initially, bank-wise limit on issue of CDs was placed at a certain percentage of the fortnightly average of outstanding aggregate deposits of 1989-90. Over time, the bank-wise limits were raised and subsequently abolished, effective on October 16, 1993, when it became a truly market determined instrument; the minimum size of issue has been lowered to Rs. 5 lakh. However, with banks offering higher interest rates on CDs, subscribes find it profitable to hold CDs till maturity; consequently, the secondary market for CDs was slow to develop.

Term Money

In order to provide some flexibility to financial institutions and also develop the term money market, select financial institutions (IDBI, ICICI, IFCI, IRBI, SIDBI, EXIM Bank and NABARD) were permitted in October 1993 to borrow from the term money market for 3-6 months maturity, within stipulated limits for each institution. Banks were exempted from the maintenance of CRR and SLR on liabilities to banking system to facilitate the development of term money market in April 1997, subject to the condition that effective CRR and SLR on total demand and time liabilities would not be less than 3 per cent and 25 per cent, respectively.

MMMFs

An initial attempt was made to make money market instruments accessible to individuals by allowing scheduled commercial banks and public financial institutions to set up MMMFs in April 1992. Despite a number of steps taken subsequently (November 1995-July 1996) to make the scheme more flexible and provide greater liquidity and depth, the response, till date, has been lukewarm, with only three funds currently operational. The Reserve Bank recently permitted MMMFs to invest in rated corporate bonds and debentures with a residual maturity of one year.

Government Paper

The Government securities market was a captive market with administered interest rates till the mid-1980s.With the rates not linked to the other money market rates no reference rate could emerge. In the absence of a transmission mechanism, the scope for active open market operations was limited. Following the implementation of the Chakravarty Committee recommendations that Treasury Bills should be developed as a monetary instrument with flexible rates for efficient management of short-term liquidity, a beginning was made with the introduction of a 182 days Treasury Bill in November 1986 on a fortnightly auction basis (the issue of fresh 182-day Treasury Bills was discontinued effective April 16, 1992).

However, it was only since 1992-93 that internal debt management was truly given a market orientation with steps taken to develop Treasury Bills as money market instruments: new instruments of 364-day auction Treasury Bills (fortnightly) and 91-day auction Treasury Bills (weekly) were introduced in April 1992 and January 1993, respectively. The 91-day auction Treasury Bill differs from the 364-day version in that, the former has a preannounced amount (which has varied in the range of Rs. 50-900 crore per auction) with likely development on the Reserve Bank. Furthermore, for the first time in 1992-93, the Central Government raised its entire gross market borrowing through the auction system. With the introduction of auctions, the coupon rates have emerged through the cut-off yield which could reflect the liquidity perception of the participants. This can be particularly gauged from the cut-off yield for 91-day auction Treasury Bills which has been significantly higher than the fixed discount rate of 4.6 per cent on its tap counterpart. The discountinuance of *ad hoc* and tap Treasury Bills, effective April 1, 1997 and introduction of auction Treasury Bills of varying maturities-viz., 14-day (effective June 6, 1997) and 28-day Treasury Bills, besides facilitating cash management of various segments of the economy, would help form a complete yield curve and thus deepen government securities market.

Recent measures include:

- Uniform price auction method in respect of 91-day Treasury Bills on an experimental basis;
- Introduction of notified amounts for auction of all securities, including Treasury Bills;
- Non-competitive bids in respect of Treasury Bills to be kept outside the notified amount.

A major step towards developing open market operations was conducting auctions of repurchase agreements (Repos) of 1-14 days for Central Government dated securities since December 1992 to even out short-term liquidity. Further, the Switch Quota facility, which was not consistent with the conduct of open market operations was discontinued effective April 1, 1992. Conduct of open market operations also needs an active secondary market where possibility of two-way quotas exist; the entry of new players like PDs and Satellite dealers (SDs) is vital in this context. As a first step in the direction of developing a secondary market in Government securities, the DFHI started dealing in Government securities, effective April 2, 1992. DFHI and STCI began functioning as PDs, effective March 1, 1996 and four more PDs became operational on June 1, 1996; these were to act as market makers for Government securities. The permission granted to FIIs to invest in Government dated securities and to banks to retail them on an outright/repos basis would further activate the government securities market. Thus, during the 1990s an array of money market instruments were developed with the supporting institutional framework.

Repo Transactions

The Reserve Bank's recent policy to allow repo transactions among banks and select entities in PSU bonds and private corporate debt securities would provide the much needed liquidity to the debt market.

III. TRENDS IN MONEY MARKET

Call Money Market

The call money market in India is very active largely due to the incidence of high cash reserve requirement on demand

and time liabilities of commercial banks. The annual turnover in call money market at Mumbai was of the order of Rs. 1,644,790 crore in 1991-92 and Rs. 1,545,160 crore in 1996-97. The turnover and the rate in the call money market generally reflected varying liquidity conditions. In this regard, the period July 1990-October 1997 can be divided into four sub-periods, depending on liquidity conditions. During July 1990-June 1992 tight liquidity conditions saw the DFHI's fortnightly average call money lending rates generally rule in double digits with a peak at 60.50 per cent in October 1990 and again at 86 per cent in April 1992. Easy liquidity conditions during July 1992-December 1994 saw the rates down except for September 1994 when the call rates had peaked at 53 per cent. This was followed by a period of tight liquidity conditions during January 1995-June 1996 with call rates soaring to 55 per cent in November 1995 largely mirroring the Reserve Bank's intervention in the forex market to stem Rupee volatility; this reflected the growing inter-linkages between the domestic call money market and the forex market. The easy liquidity conditions in the subsequent period saw rates rule in single digits. Other money market rates also reflect the liquidity conditions.

Commercial Paper

Commercial paper, as a money market instrument, has proved to be popular in India, primarily during periods of downswing in credit growth, enabling corporates to access the CP market at rates lower than PLR of banks. The amount of commercial paper (CP) issued by corporates increased significantly from Rs. 577 crore in March 1993 to reach a historical peak of Rs. 4,511 crore in August 1994 along side a decline in the average discount rate from 15.88 per cent to 10.50 per cent during this period. With the firming up of call money rates, the average effective discount rate touched peak of 20.15 per cent in April 1996 with concomitant decline in outstanding amount of CPs which touched a historical low of Rs. 71 crore. The subsequent easing of liquidity conditions resulted in the renewed interest towards issue of commercial paper and the outstanding amount of CPs increased to Rs. 3,811 crore in September 1997.

Certificates of Deposit (CDs)

The variation in the issue of certificates of deposit (CDs) by scheduled commercial banks during July 1990-July 1997 broadly reflected, the liqudity trends of the economy. It may be indicated that CDs are relatively high cost deposits and gain in importance during the upswing of credit cycle. The outstanding amount of CDs expanded from Rs. 2,000 crore in July 1990 to Rs. 12,557 crore as on July 1993. As liquidity conditions eased the outstanding amount of CDs and the effective discount rate declined to Rs. 5,218 crore and to 10.75 per cent, respectively in July 1994. As the demand for bank credit accelerated, the outstanding amount of CDs increased steadily to scale a historical peak of Rs. 21,503 crore in June 1996 and the average interest rate increased to 15.5-17.0 per cent during January-June 1996. As liquidity conditions eased, the outstanding amount of CDs and the average interest rate declined to Rs. 8,850 crore and to 10.6 per cent, respectively, in July 1997.

91-day Auction Treasury Bills

The variation in the implicit cut-off yield of 91-day Auction Treasury Bills has reflected apart from the changing liquidity conditions, (i) changes in the notified amount, (ii) development in the Reserve Bank and the PDs, (iii) participation of non-competitive bidders, etc. Hence, the cut-off yield for the instrument is market related rather than market determined. The cut-off yield declined steadily from 11.10 per cent to 7.21 per cent during the period of easy liquidity between April 1993 and May 1994. Reflecting hardening of money market rates, the implicit cut-off yield increased steadily to peak at 12.97 per cent during November 1995-April 1996. The cut-off yield exhibited a steady decline to 5.72 per cent a historical low–on April 17, 1997. It has since remained under 7 per cent, reflecting easy liquidity conditions.

364-day Auction Treasury Bills

The cut-off yield on 364-day Auction Treasury Bills and the outstanding amount of 364-day Treausry Bills, introduced in April 1992, are better indicators of liquidity conditions—in the absence of notified amount and development on the Reserve

Bank–than those of 91-day Auction Treasury Bills. The outstanding amount of 364-day Treasury Bills increased from Rs. 8,797 crore as at end-March 1993 to an all time high of Rs. 20,323 crore by mid-March 1994 which prompted the government to convert Bills amounting to about Rs. 11,937 crore into dated government security. The outstanding amount again scaled a high of about Rs. 19,291 crore in mid-August 1994 causing a second round of conversion of about Rs. 8,694 crore. The outstanding amount of 364-day Treasury Bills declined to Rs. 1,875 crore as at end-March 1996, despite an increase in the cut-off yield to a historical peak of 13.12 per cent. Evidently, the market participants had lost interest in this instrument as other avenues—particularly, expansion of non-food bank credit—became more attractive to banks in a tight money situation. As credit expansion decelerated, there was a renewed interest for 364-day Treasury Bills with the outstanding amount increasing to Rs. 15,511 crore as at end-September 1997 with attendant decline in cut-off yield to 8.47 per cent.

CONCLUSION

The Indian money market was circumscribed by tight controls and administered interest rate structure up to the late 1980s. However, following the policy measures during the early 1990s the money market has become broad based with enlargement of participants and instruments, and change in liquidity conditions is quickly transmitted. The reform measures have greatly contributed to the development of inter-linkages; indicating liquidity pass-through across various segments of the money market. An enabling environment has thus been created whereby the monetary authority can gradually switch away from the direct instruments of monetary control to indirect methods like the open market operations, including repos. The market determined interest rate is gradually emerging as an important intermediate target with the ultimate objective of achieving price stability and economic growth. This process is aided by the reactivisation of the Bank Rate to serve as a 'signaling rate' to the market about the monetary authority's liquidity perceptions so as to influence market behaviour. Recent developments in the call money market also indicate a growing inter linkage between the domestic money market and the forex market. With a move towards capital account convertibility, the links will be strengthened further.

On use of money market instruments by central banks a study of six East Asian economies by Emery (1992) reveals that success in controlling liquidity depends on employing money market instruments that have yields based on actual market demand and supply. Hence, further steps need to be taken to dismantle the remnants of the administered interest rate regime and further deepen and widen the secondary market subject to proper safeguardss to prevent systemic crises. Further, in a cross-country perspective Kneesaw and Van den Bergh (1989) observed that government debt management has often constrained money market operations. In India also, open market operations were rendered impotent till recently; with the reduction in fiscal deficit and surge in capital inflows, open market operations (including sterilisation) is gaining renewed significance to control liquidity. However, there still exists many areas where reforms towards furthering financial market integration need to be carried out by enlarging money market participation, giving it greater depth and liquidity.

References

Axilrod, S.H. (1996)—*Transformations to Open Market Operations, Developing Economies and Emerging Markets,* International Monetary Fund, Washington, D.C.

Chawla, O.P. (ed.) (1990)—*Money and Securities Markets,* National Institute of Bank Management, Pune.

Cole, D.C., H.S. Scott, and P.A. Wellons (eds.) (1995)—*Asian Money Markets,* Oxford University Press, New York.

Emery, R.F. (1992)—*Central Banks' Use in East Asia of Money Market Instruments in the Conduct of Monetary Policy,* Board of Governors of the Federal Reserve System, International Finance Discussion Papers: 426.

Kneeshaw, J.T., and Van den Bergh (1989)—*Changes in Central Bank Money Market Operating Procedures in the 1980s,* BIS Economic Papers, No. 23, Basel.

Oularis, S. (1995)—"An Econometric Analysis of Asian Money Markets" in Cole, D.C., H.S. Scott and P.A. Wellons (eds.): *Asian Money Markets,* Oxford University Press, New York.

Reserve Bank of India—*Annual Report,* Various issues, Mumbai.

Reserve Bank of India (1985)—*Report of the Committee to Review the Working of the Monetary System,* Bombay.

Reserve Bank of India (1987)—*Report of the Working Group on the Money Market*, Bombay.

Stigum, M. (1990)—*The Money Market*, Business One Irwin, Homewood, Illinois.

Wilson, J.S.G. (1993)—*Money Markets: The International Perspective*, Routledge, London and New York.

PART B

MONEY AND CAPITAL MARKET INTERACTIONS

4

Stock Market Adjustments to Policy Changes

T.V.S. Rammohan Rao

1. THE QUESTIONS

Efficient financial markets have the role of catalysts. They channel the saving in the economy into productive investment activity on the basis of the strength of the market demand for various goods and services. For all practical purposes this financial intermediation sustains the growth path of the economy. The real economic activity leads the changes in the availability of financial resources in this framework. Shortage of financial resources may, however, retard the growth process.[1]

On occasions there are suggestions that if the money and financial markets are buoyant there will be well meaning entrepreneurs who will put into operation worthwhile real activity which they would hesitate to take up otherwise. In this approach the financial sector leads real economic activity.[2]

Following the economic reforms initiated in 1991 and the associated market oriented liberalization policies there have been short spells of significant increases in the stock prices. At least some optimists suggest that there has been a steady upward trend due to the positive effect of financial reforms on the market fundamentals and real growth in the gross domestic product. However, recent empirical studies—such as Chatarath *et. al.* (1995), Amanulla *et. al.* (1996), Murty (1996), and Shah and Thomas (1997)—indicate that this is not the case. Two questions are therefore pertinent: (1) Is there any rational economic explanation for the inability of the financial reforms to bring about a growth in the real economic activity?; (2) What are the tangible gains, if any, of the liberalization process set in motion? A somewhat heuristic analysis will be attempted in this study.

The rest of the paper is organized as follows: Section 2 develops the theoretical argument. The effects of policy changes will be outlined in section 3. Section 4 offers some basic empirical facts to support the contentions of this study. Some policy implications are outlined in section 5.

2. THE ANALYTICAL STRUCTURE

The demand for the common stock of a firm consists of at least three components:[3] (1) The share prices will be determined by the underlying profitability of an investment and the expected rates of return. In general, it can be argued that a greater volume of shares will be demanded only at a lower price (which represents a higher rate of return). This is depicted as D_i in Fig. 1 *Datt and Sundaram* (1996, p. 755) label this as the investment demand. (2) There is always some speculative activity in the stock market. As Datt and Sundaram (1996, p. 755) pointed out, this is an indicator of stock market liquidity which, in its turn, is the basic precondition to ensure that the fluctuations in the stock prices portray the changes in the real economic activity. In Fig. 1, D_s is the sum of D_i and the speculative demand.[4] (3) It is well-known that the need to finance the fiscal deficit of the government by the sale of treasury bills resulted in channeling saving away from the capital market. An extreme situation can be visualized wherein finances are not available to undertake D_1. By the same token it is also possible that if there is an excessive saving in the economy there will be an excess supply in the financial markets and it

FIG. 1
Stock Price Determination

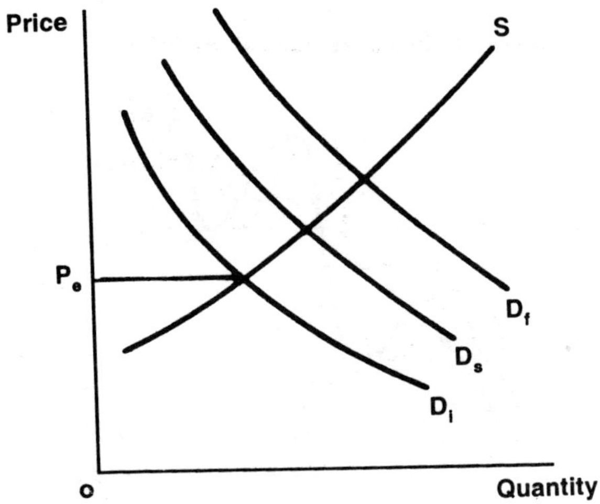

may be dissipated in the form of speculative activity if there are supply constraints on the productive sectors. D is the total demand[5] when this component is added to D_s.

The supply of common stock depends on three basic forces: (1) The investment demand as calibrated by the profit generating potential[6] and/or the actual payments to the shareholders in the form of dividends, (2) the availability and the costs of various sources of financing, and (3) the transaction costs involved in the use of different financial instruments.[7] The demand, by firms, for stock market financing is determined by these considerations. Let S in Fig. 1 denote the supply of common stock. The effect of policy instruments can be traced through appropriate shifts in S as well.

For all practical purposes the intersection of D_i and S represents the intrinsic price of common stock based on investment fundamentals embodied in the real economic activity. See, for instance, Murty (1996, p. 36). P_e in Fig. 1 indicates the efficient market price of common stock.[8]

Suppose, for analytical purposes, that there is an improvement in the real activity. This can be expected to shift

D_i to the right and increase P_e. In other words, an upward trend in p_e in the long run, as in Fig. 2, is expected even if there are speculative bubbles around it in the short run. This feature alone signals economic progress.

FIG. 2

Stock Price and Real Activities

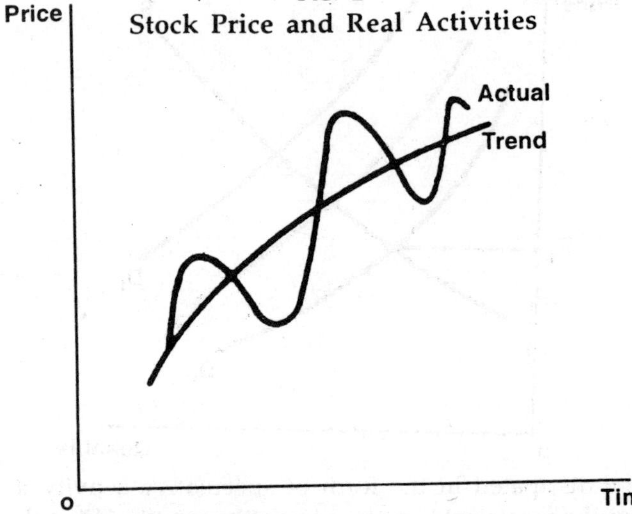

One qualification is in order. As D_i shifts to the right it will be expected that S will also shift to the right albeit with a time lag.[9] The resulting change in P_e will still be an increase though of a smaller magnitude. To expect S to lead D_i appears unrealistic. In general, a healthy real growth of the economy can be expected to result in an upward trend in p_e.

It is now evident that the changes in policy instruments of the government and/or the Reserve Bank of India affect the D and/or the S and thereby the stock prices. The pertinent question is: which of these policies affect stock prices through their effect on the fundamentals of the real economic activity? The next section attempts a brief analysis of this issue.

3. POLICY CHANGES

The saving of individuals is collected by the financial system primarily through three institutional arrangements: (1) the stock market, (2) non-bank financial intermediaries like the UTI (and other mutual funds) and LIC, and (3) the banking system. Individual investors constitute a small portion of the traders on the stock market. The basic reason for this is the excessive transaction costs. Most of the finances tend to be diverted to the stock market via the financial institutions. Even they tend to concentrate on an inner core of holdings of the shares of the largest companies. The high transaction costs explain this choice as well. There are very few good floating scrips and the stock market liquidity is low. Even so there was enough money available and stocks like that of Metal Box were quoted at high prices despite their low intrinsic rate of return, (Datt and Sundaram, 1996, p. 763). When the households deposit their saving with a bank they can in turn provide finances to the firms through the debt route. However, with the increasing fiscal deficit and the need to finance it through appropriate open market operations in treasury bills, the banks are being forced to utilize a large fraction of deposits and loanable funds to fulfil their SLR and CRR requirements. Similarly, a part of the available finances are channeled to less than satisfactory priority sector lending. The role of banks in promoting investments is therefore rather circumscribed.

Despite this it appears that there is a surplus of saving chasing too few good stocks on the capital market. Three observations are pertinent in this context: (1) whenever a new issue is floated there is a manifold over subscription leading to a necessity to ration the available shares. (2) Despite the high interest rates on debt financing companies resort to its use as the first priority due to lower transaction costs and such finances are available despite all the arguments about the liquidity crunch. (3) During the early stages of the reform, e.g., in 1992-93 some banks made a large amount of funds available to selected brokers (read Harshad Mehta). They cornered the limited floating shares of leading companies like the ACC and Reliance and pushed up their prices.[10]

Three, conclusions are therefore pertinent: (1) There is an excess supply of saving to the stock market in relation to the fundamental strengths and investment requirements. (2) Despite the excess supply the interest rates did not decrease primarily due to high government borrowing and the need to reduce the recovery risks involved in priority sector lending. (3) Most of the observed increases in stock prices are due to speculative demand rather than improved market fundamentals.

Consider the problems of money market liquidity due to the RBI regulations on the banking sector. The effect is of a short term nature and perhaps did not allow firms to recover potential returns. However, since long term finances were available and could be diverted to finance working capital, *albeit* at an increased cost, the negative effect on the stock market was perhaps marginal, if any.

The role of the non-bank financial intermediaries and foreign institutional investors is also dubious. They merely provide the individual investors a means of consolidating their risks.

However, given the segmented and inefficient capital market their role is merely speculative. They made attempts to utilize the arbitrage possibilities to make profits. Two observations will justify this inference: (1) When the product market fundamentals disciplined the investors stock prices fell sharply and institutional investors like the UTI suffered substantially because they were speculating in the first instance. (Recall their experiences with Reliance and ACC.) (2) Most of the foreign deposits were withdrawn soon after an increase in interest rates in the U.S.A. and Germany. In fact, due to the non-convertibility of the rupee even small changes were sufficient to induce a flight of capital.

The only positive contribution to increases in stock prices may have come from foreign direct investments, especially in the infrastructure sector. The lack of full convertibility of the rupee did not deter them. As such it is an indication that they expect tangible real returns on such investments.

Even when the liberalization process was set in motion or a withdrawal of MAT was announced in the recent budget there was an excess (speculative) demand for shares and the stock prices went up. However, in the short run such measures do not alter product market fundamentals, profitable investments, and the purchase of capital assets by firms. The stock price bubble bursts sooner than later.

On the contrary the recent announcements of direct tax reductions may have the effect of increasing expenditure on consumer goods and improving capacity expansion in related goods thereby increasing the real returns on such investments. The stock market may again show an upward trend if the exsting saving is chanelled to make productive investments in this sector.

One may wonder as to what the tangible gains of the financial and banking sector reforms have been. The answer is simply that the turnover will increase thereby signalling a greater stock market liquidity and a movement toward more efficient capital market integration.

In view of this analysis three trends should be discernible: (1) After 1992 there is no appreciable uptrend in stock prices. (2) The growth in the primary issues is not commensurate with the growth in GDP or the growth of the industrial sector. (3) The turnover on the stock exchanges has increased though even this is not a sustained progress. These empirical facts will be documented in the next section.

4. EMPIRICAL FACTS

The experiences with economic reforms span only 1992-96. As such it is rather difficult to make any definitive claims about the patterns of economic progress and their causative factors. However, the following evidence is sufficiently persuasive.

Consider Fig. 3. The BSE sensitive index does not exhibit any positive trend. Instead, it hovers around 3400. The two upswings—one in early 1992 and the other in 1994-95 are merely reflections of the speculative expectations generated by political changes. The downturns were caused by the disappointments in the power sector (Enron contract) and the communications sector (where firms like HFCL could not justify their bids by raising adequate project finance.)[11]

Somewhat more systematic analysis by Chatarath *et. al.* (1995), Amanulla *et. al.* (1996), and Murty (1996) also revealed that the real economic activity (represented by the index of industrial production) did not have any influence on the stock prices.[12]

Both Amanulla *et. al.* (1996) and Murty (1996) also examined the effect of changes in money supply (M1 and M3 respectively). As Murty (1996, p. 142) concluded, the "results indicate that the market could not anticipate the three month movements in money supply and was reacting to short term movements with

FIG. 3

BSE Sensex of Share Prices

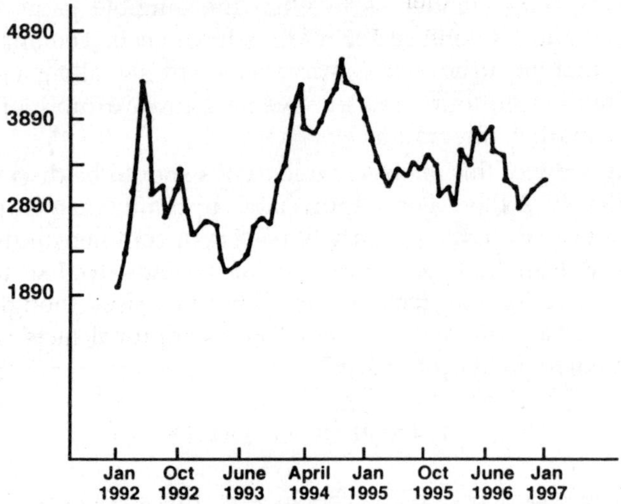

Source : Economic Survey, 96-97, p. 60.

a lag of about half a month to a month. (This implies) that the . . . . stock market is not efficient."

The figures pertaining to new issues is presented in Fig. 4. It can be reasonably inferred that upto 94-95 there was an upward trend though by the end of 1995, the implementation of the Malegam Committee recommendations—that companies with post-issue equity of less than Rs. 5 crores cannot float public issues—created a severe downturn. If it is assumed that there was no excess supply to begin with and the preferences for equity financing did not change by very much, the trend in the new issues must correspond to the growth in industrial production. It is difficult to sustain this on the basis of the evidence available in Fig. 4. In general, some gains have been made in the real economic activity and the new issues absorbed excess supply and reduced speculative deals.[13] However, it cannot be claimed that industrial progress depended entirely on the stock market.

Consider Fig. 5 in which the quarterly turnover on the

BSE has been presented. It is fairly clear that there has been a steady upward trend despite the high seasonal variability represented by the conventional busy and slack seasons of real economic activity. It would be reasonable to conclude that there was an increase in stock market liquidity.

FIG. 4

Capital Issues in the Primary Market

(Rs. 100 Crores)

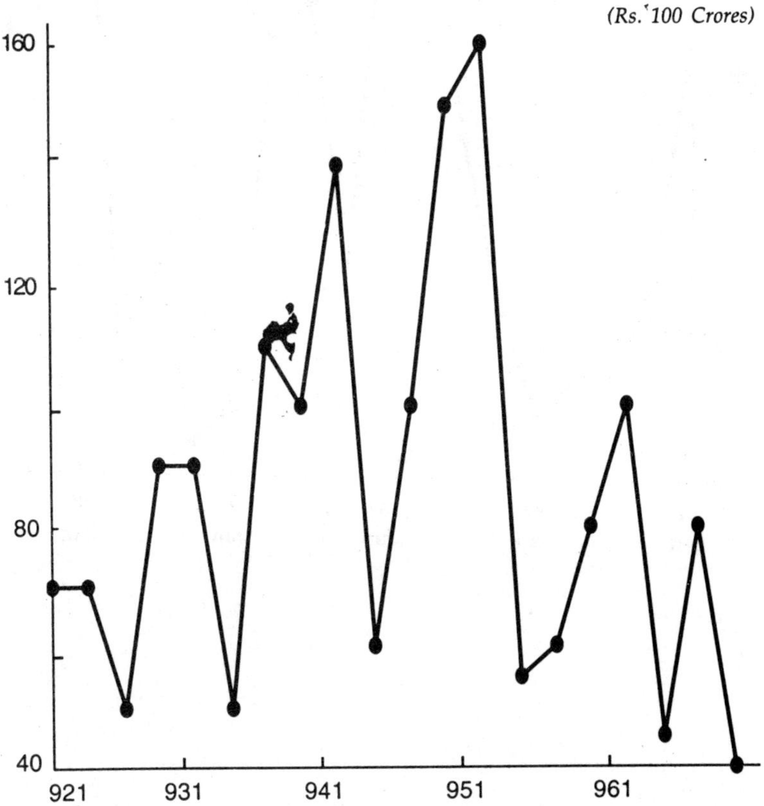

Source : CMIE, *Capital Issues*, January 1997, p. 20.

FIG. 5

Quarterly Turnover on the BSE

(Rs. 100 Crores)

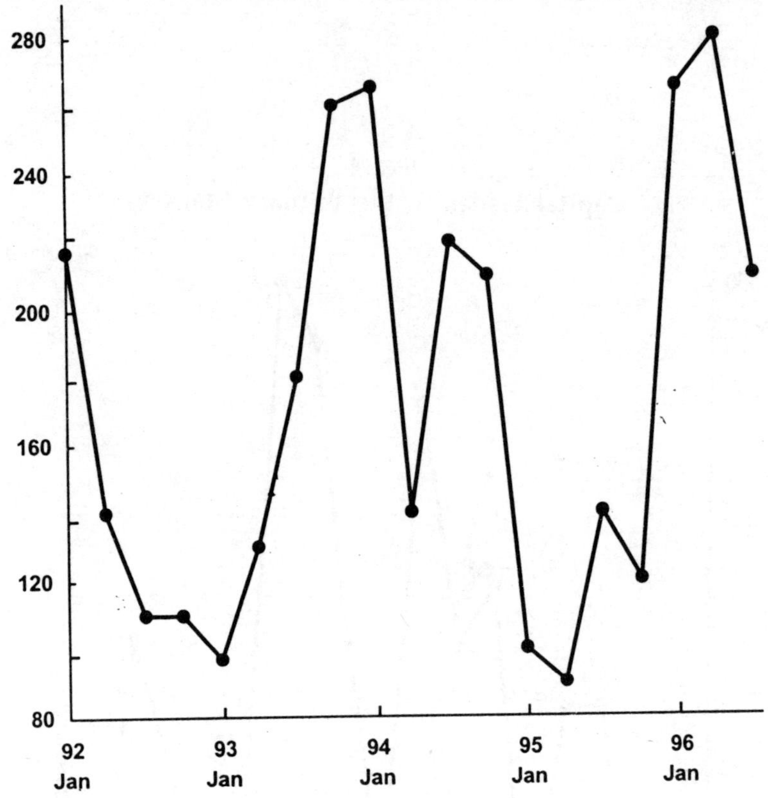

Source: CMIE : *Capital Markets*, January 1997, p. 151.

The following conclusions are pertinent. (1) Fundamentally there is an excess of saving in the economy which is dissipated in the form of speculative activity on the stock market. This is the basic reason for the observed spurts in stock prices as well as the inability of the stock market to sustain such increases. (2) Stock market liquidity and the increase in the volume of transactions is the only tangible gain from the reforms in the financial sector. In other words, there is a movement towards greater efficiency of the financial markets. To be sure, this is a necessary condition for real economic progress.

5. SOME POLICY IMPLICATIONS

The inadequacy of physical infrastructure (power, communications) and the inability of the economy to overcome this barrier is the real reason behind the sluggish growth process. In general, profitable investment opportunities are rather few despite the enormous market potential which has been cited by the multinationals so often. As Rao and Sinha (1996) argued, the reform process has yet to come to grips with setting up the requisite enabling institutions and control processes.

The government took up the role of investor for too long. Even so it did not have adequate finances to fulfill the investment needs of the infrastructure sector. The surplus generating potential of the public enterprises has been very low. This is a part of the difficulty in controlling fiscal deficits. Obviously, there is a recognition that this cannot continue much longer.

Significant fiscal deficits and their financing through monetary changes increased money supply and kept the interest rates high. The resulting excessive saving spilled over into the capital market and created unproductive speculation and an impression that the real returns from the stock market are commensurate with the real earnings from the money market. It has not been possible to sustain this illusion since the fundamentals pertaining to the real economic activity are not very strong. There is no short cut to trimming government spending and reducing fiscal deficits if efficiency and integration has to be brought about in the financial markets. The interest rates will reduce automatically if this process of adaptation succeeds.

On the whole, it can be concluded that changes in money supply and the flow of funds to the financial markets can only have a supporting role. They cannot alter the product market fundamentals. Economic policies to encourage new capital investsments, especially in sectors where there is an enormous potential demand, is the basic necessity. However, this is not taken up sincerely. The financial reforms, directed towards greater efficiency and instilling investor confidence, are necessary to ensure that the real economic growth is not stifled. The progress made in this direction is worthwhile though it is not a sufficient condition. The speculative bubbles in stock market prices should be reduced to the minimum necessary for its efficient functioning and should not be misinterpreted as indicating increases in real economic growth.

Notes and References

1. See, for instance, Gurley and Shaw (1966, ch. 4).
2. Some early work, on what has come to be designated as the St. Louis equation, argued that changes in the money supply rather than government expenditures lead the changes in real economic activity. See, for instance, Keran (1971). This may be plausible if there is an excess productive capacity *a priori*. The argument is not equally valid in a supply constrained economy. However, a test of causality has not been conducted so far.
3. It is perhaps reasonable to argue that no seperate conceptualization is necessary for the primary and secondary markets for these instruments. For, both the components of demand depend on product market fundamentals. Further, the rates of return in both these markets will be the same if the capital market is efficient.
4. The position of D_s with respect to D_i clearly depends on the relative strength of the bulls and the bears on the market.
5. It is worthwhile to note two points in this context: (1) The demand for a given volume of common stock has an equivalent in terms of the supply of finances. The analysis can be conducted in such a framework as well. (2) The demand for stocks and shares in the aggregate setting will not be unitary elastic. Instead, it can be expected that the volume of money committed to the stock market increases at higher rates of growth.
6. Note that a discrepancy between the profit expectations of the management and the shareholders is not ruled out. An efficient market attempts to align these expectations.
7. In the recent literature there is a recognition that there can be a shortage of money market liquidity. That is, the bank credit to finance short

term working capital may be limited. (It should be noted paranthetically that stock market liquidity denotes the frequency with which a given stock is traded on the secondary market. As such money market liquidity has a different connotation). In such a case it may not be possible to undertake even profitable investments. See Fazzari and Petersen (1993) and Sastry and Kelkar (1997).

8. To be sure the procedural and institutional details which increase fairness, and transperancy, and reduce transaction costs may increase or at least stabilize the share prices.
9. This is the position of Friedman (1988, pp. 222-3) based on empirical evidence. As he puts it, a *ceteris paribus* increase in the real economic activity causes an excess demand for investment instruments. In turn, the increase in the demand for common stock results in an upward movement of the share prices. The wealth effect implicit in such growth increases the demand for real balances. Money supply should increase to sustain this growth process. They reverse causation was expected in some earlier literature. See, for instance, Keran (1971). It appears that Friedman's argument is more plausible *a priori.*
10. It must be recognized that the companies themselves are in no way accountable to the price movements in the secondary markets. From the viewpoint of investor safety that should be expected to curb unjustifiable speculation.
11. In general, there was a feeling that the implementation of the reforms was inefficient and half-hearted.
12. However, firms (even those belonging to the small size B and B2 groups) such as Eicher ,performed well because of strong demand.
13. Augustine *et. al.* (1997, p. 59) pointed out that large excess capacities in several major companies meant that the product market expansion did not necessitate new capital investments and hence new issues of shares.

References

Amanulla, S., A.K. Giri, and B. Kamiah (1996): Information Arrivals. Stock Price Variability, and Market Efficiency in Indian Stock Market, *Arthavijana*, 38, 20-33.

Augustine, B.D., N. Datt, and U. Seth (1997): Winners and Losers, *Business India*, January 12, 58-63.

Chatrath, A., S. Ramachandran, and F. Song (1995): Real Activity, Stock Prices, and Inflation, *Indian Economic Journal*, 43, 86-96.

CMIE (1997): *Capital Markets*, January.

Datt, R. and K.P.M. Sundharam (1996): *Indian Economy*, S. Chand, New Delhi.

Fazzari, S.M. and B.C. Petersen (1993): Working Capital and Fixed Investsment: New Evidence on Financing Constraints, *Rand Journal of Economics*, 24, 328-342.

Friedman, M. (1988): Money and the Stock Market, *Journal of Political Economy*, 96, 221-245.

GOI (1997): *Economic Survey 1996-97,* Ministry of Finance, New Delhi.

Gurley, J.G. and E.S. Shaw (1966): *Money in a Theory of Finance,* Brookings Institution, Washington.

Keran, M.W. (1971): Expectations, Money, and the Stock Market, *Federal Reserve Bank of St. Louis Review,* 53, 16-32.

Murty, Y.S.R. (1996): Stock Prices, Money, Inflation and Real Activity: A Cross-Spectral View, *Arthavijana,* 38, 34-64.

Rao, T.V.S.R. and S. Sinha (1996): Industrial Infrastructure in the Reform Process, *Indian Journal of Economics,* 77, 89-106.

Sastry, D.V.S. and U.R. Kelkar (1997): Working Capital and Fixed Investment—Financing Constraints, Presented at the Indian Econometric Society Meetings, Hyderabad, March.

Shah, A. and S. Thomas (1997): Securities Markets: Towards Greater Efficiency, K.S. Parikh (ed.) *India Development Report* 1997. Oxford University Press, 1997.

5

Capital Market in India—The Role of Commercial Banks

A.J. Chakraborty

For the last couple of years, particularly from the implementation of the economic reform policy (i.e. New Economic Policy NEP of 1991) by the Government of India, spectacular changes in the banking industry started taking place. This new economic policy is usually segregated into: (i) Stabilisation Policy, and (ii) Structural Adjustment Policy. The financial markets have major role to play in achieving desired results in both of the components. This is why the Narasimham Committee has made important recommendations for reforms and overall changes particularly, in the orientation and performance of commercial banks. The avowed objectives of course are higher productivity, profitability, efficiency and competitive.

This paper wants to examine the following issues. First, it tries to ascertain the role of commercial banks in the Indian economy's capital market. For that matter it first : (i) shows the importance of banks and the shortcomings associated with it, and (ii) it examines the extent of reforms that have taken in this context and the deficiency related in this context. Secondly, it pinpoints the major obstacles Indian commercial banking sector faces. In this connection, the paper also examines the feasibility of implementing the recommendations of the Narasimham Committee. Third the paper suggest some further policies consistent with the Committee's report especially in the area of management of assets, liquidity, so as to be the most active actor in the Indian capital market. In this connection, it may be noted that capital market is concerned with the promotion of savings and investment and efficient allocation of long term funds among competing uses. It is the function of the capital market to convert private savings, individual as well as corporate, into investments through new capital issues and also new public loans floated by government and semi-government organisations. It is often said that in recent times the Indian banking system is on the threshold of the second banking revolution after the first in 1969—in the sense that a major thrust have taken to achieve viability and efficiency of this sector. This simply because the productive sectors of the economy can operate efficiently provided the banking system also operates efficiently by transfering funds from surplus units to deficit units. The Indian banking system is the major actor in the field of capital markets in Indian economy with large geographical and diverse areas of functioning. However, there has been a growing concern about the viability and efficiency of the Indian banking system as actor in capital market. For example, the interest income as a percentage of average working fund was 9.5% in the year 1992-93, while the interest cost plus the other cost accounts 9.75%, thus there is a loss of 0.25% of average working fund. One major reason which is often cited is that the Indian banking system became a victim of anti-competitive philosophy. This is why the Narasimham Committee gave major thrust in re-structuring entirely on the commercial banking to meet the challenges of competitive financial system more effectively. So long commercial banks acted in sellers market and the lending policies it followed was called rationing approach is going to be replaced into a buyers market, where better credit rated clients have several options and are demanding funds on much softer terms. So long bulk of the resources mobilized by banks were pre-empted by the R.B.I./ G.O.I. through ever increasing levels of SLR and CRR, priority sector lending, food credit etc. It thus created shortage of funds available for discretionary lending by the banks. Now there is a change, the banks have been given liberty and flexibility, so that, it can maximise income through a sound asset management portfolio. Here, therefore comes the role of banks in the capital market in the economy. Now the opportunity set has been enlarged. The bank now must prudently learn the acquisition of the composition of their assets, i.e. marketable assets in response to the changing situations.

A change is the activities of the banks in the capital market has been noticed very recently. The banks are now moving away from cash credit system and favouring lending through bills scheme of flotation of commercial paper. Instead of giving term loans it is now trying to invest in debentures of various maturities. As noted by Patil,[4] banks are now taking advantage of the debt trading facilities made available by N.S.E. by persuading their clients to rely increasingly on marketable instruments. This lending route is likely to give considerable degree of freedom to banks to re-arrange of portfolio as per their needs. Now banks did not hold large cash because as they can always create liquidity by selling assets on the market.

DEVELOPMENT IN THE AREA OF COMMERCIAL BANKS SINCE 1991

Scarcity of loanable fund was one of the major problems of commercial banks. The Narasimham Committee suggested progressive reduction of the then existing CRR and SLR to augment supply of credit from commercial banks. It also suggested some additional methods in this respect, e.g., increase in the ceiling of investment for shares, securities and public sector bonds to enables banks to increase income thereof. Some innovative suggestions were also there, e.g. banks entrance in new type of business· i.e. leasing, hire purchase, factoring, housing finance, consultancy, trading in shares and securities etc. for increasing income.

Increased thrust given to export sector by government to enable banks to increase their lending to this 'sunrise sector' for earning higher income. Though corporate sectors demand for funds on banks decreases due to dis-intermediation, banks can successfully increase their lending to trade, commerce and SSI sector and loans to individuals for consumer durables and housing. As agricultural sector is going to act more specialised, opportunity exists for commercial banks in view of their large network at rural and semi-urban centres. Food-processing, agro-based industries, aquaculture, horticulture and floriculture have been identified by government as thrust areas and they are attracting the interests of foreign investment bankers. Banks can quote competitive rates when demand for credit goes up and can quote not to attractive rates when saddled with a position of surplus funds. Banks can maximise deposit mobilisation by following different interest rate at different centres or branches by way of price differentiation.

High-rated corporates are now directly acquiring funds from domestic or international capital market. This dis-intermediation forced banks to lend technologically backward and they faced high competition in respect of price and quality; so to compete with the manufacturers in domestic markets they often tie-up with foreign collaborators. This may adversely affect the asset portfolio of banks. Again, progressive liberalisation in trade sector would result in further reduction in customs duty which may encourage imports of finished goods jeopardising the interest of the import intensive industries and adversely affect the asset portfolio of commercial banks.

Commercial banks could not utilize their whole deposit fund in their own discretion, because out of their deposit they have to maintain CRR, cash in vault ratio, SLR etc. and also they have to make considerable advances to priority sectors, like, agriculture, small scale industries etc. In case of public sector bank percentage of priority sector advances to total bank credit was 45% (June '87). Unrestricted credit in this priority sector brought serious losses and instability to the whole banking sector.

Commercial banks could not mobilize deposit efficiently due to the development of capital market in recent years, growth in the non-banking financial sector and increase in awareness amongst investors. Investors are now ready to bear more risks for anticipated higher return and therefore they prefer corporate securities than bank deposits. Demand for bank advances from corporate sector have been reduced due to increase in the investment from the foreign institutional investors. In order to be competitively efficient the Narasimham Committee suggested greater participation by the commercial banks in both primary and secondary capital markets. However, the last "scam" and the style of handling this case have raised much doubts and virtually rationed strictly if not prevented banks participation in the emerging capital markets. The political compulsion has thus appeared a strong hurdle to bank's enlarged role in the capital markets.

A bank's performance can be measured from its capacity to manage total liabilities and allocation of total liability fund to different assets. Profitability is the main target of banks, so to minimise cost they try to determine their profitable mix of liabilities and to maximise revenue they determine the profitable mix of assets.

While assessing the performance of commercial bank we have to compare between them the performance indicators e.g. percentage of deposits, borrowings, advances, investments etc. to working funds, cash-deposit (CD) ratio, return on advances and investments, net profit etc. Let us have a brief look over some important components of performance appraisals.

Management of Liability

Commercial banks are low capital based. From Table 1 it can be observed that percentage of own funds to working funds is only 2.98%. The major source of asset creation for banks is raising resources by mobilization of deposits through time deposits (i.e. fixed deposit) and demand deposit (i.e. savings and current account). From Table 1, it can be observed that private sector Indian banks mobilize highest deposits (86.29%) while foreign banks are the lowest (67.03%). CD ratio highly affect bank borrowings. From Table 2 it can be observed that out of all nationalised banks Indian bank has highest CD ratio (67.45%) and therefore also has highest percentage of borrowings to working funds (12.46%). In case of New Bank of India which have lowest CD ratio (41.26%) and therefore their percentage of borrowings to working funds is 2nd lowest (1.42%).

Other liabilities includes Bills payable, Draft payable etc. and banks does not pay more attention to manage these types of liabilities.

TABLE 1

Assets and Liabilities of all Scheduled Commercial Banks, 1992-93 as percentage of Working Funds

	SBI Group	*Nationalised Banks*	*Public Sector Banks*	*Private Sector Indian Banks*	*Foreign Banks*	*Private Sector Banks*	*Total*
Liabilities							
Own Funds	1.79	3.31	2.75	2.52	5.75	4.57	2.98
Deposits :	68.39	85.29	79.03	86.29	67.03	74.02	78.39
Fixed	38.33	55.24	48.98	55.45	52.46	53.54	49.56
SB	13.56	17.87	16.27	16.48	4.30	8.72	15.31
Current	16.50	12.18	13.78	14.36	10.27	11.76	13.52
Borrowings	10.46	4.42	6.66	4.36	20.50	14.65	7.67
Other Liab. and Prov.	19.36	6.98	11.56	6.83	6.72	6.76	10.96
Total	100.00	100.00	100.00	100.00	100.00	100.00	100.00
Assets							
Cash on Hand	0.39	0.89	0.71	2.05	0.16	0.85	0.72
Balance with RBI	8.72	9.35	9.11	12.97	11.56	12.07	9.49
Balance with Banks	0.52	3.00	2.08	3.83	3.67	3.73	2.29
Money at Call and Short Notice	1.75	1.22	1.42	1.57	1.65	1.62	1.45
Investments	28.25	31.07	30.02	28.44	36.34	33.47	30.46
Advances:	47.31	45.35	46.08	44.80	33.85	37.83	45.03
B/P or B/D	4.57	5.69	5.27	7.55	6.98	7.19	5.52
CC/OD	31.40	26.09	28.06	26.07	19.62	21.96	27.28
Term Loans	11.34	13.57	12.75	11.18	7.25	8.68	12.23
Other Assets	13.06	9.12	10.58	6.34	12.77	10.43	10.58
Total	100.00	100.00	100.00	100.00	100.00	100.00	100.00

Management of Banking Assets

Investment management is synonymous with the SLR management, since investments made by Commercial Banks is dependent on the SLR fixed by the RBI. From Table 1, it can be observed that percentage of investment to working funds is highest in case of foreign banks (36.34%) and lowest in case

TABLE 2

Nationalised Banks, 1992-93

Nationalised Banks	Working Funds (Rs. in lac)	% of Dep. to wkg. funds	% of Borr. to wkg. funds	% Cost of Dep. to Borr.	% of Adv. to wkg. funds	CD Ratio $\left(\frac{Adv.}{Dep.} x100\right)$	Return on Adv.	% of Inv. to wkg. funds	% of Return on Inv.	Operating profit (Rs. in lac)	Net profit (Rs. in lac)
Canara	2048177	80.39	9.91	7.72	39.26	48.84	13.60	38.00	10.98	46156	2607
Baroda	2406325	87.19	3.41	7.92	48.97	56.17	13.70	26.53	9.40	34316	823
PNB	2110638	86.43	3.60	8.09	46.98	54.36	11.71	34.48	11.06	25843	3801
Indian	1475980	77.75	12.46	9.28	52.45	67.45	12.58	26.04	11.00	11211	651
India	2317818	84.21	4.28	8.12	49.84	59.18	10.72	24.03	10.52	10801	-33112
Union	1033033	90.11	1.38	8.00	43.42	48.18	11.86	34.23	10.43	7047	1126
Oriental	474292	90.80	2.57	8.17	46.79	51.53	12.69	32.90	10.34	5637	2050
Corporation	317417	89.90	4.13	6.96	38.37	43.24	12.50	34.06	10.39	4783	412
Vijaya	376397	87.86	3.40	8.09	42.64	48.53	12.71	33.66	9.52	398	-9788
Dena	496495	83.46	1.80	8.12	40.03	47.97	12.42	33.69	9.94	292	-9046
Allahabad	892415	86.20	2.29	9.42	44.33	51.43	12.88	33.74	9.23	60	-10589
Andhra	474017	88.37	2.76	8.32	40.25	45.54	11.99	31.63	10.01	-3411	-14109
IOB	10788441	88.15	1.62	8.28	49.83	56.53	7.71	28.37	9.91	-4633	-75274
Central	1547165	89.35	1.63	8.68	44.01	49.26	12.40	33.56	10.02	-4982	-38331
Maha	468939	82.61	2.29	8.73	39.55	47.87	11.16	34.70	9.77	-5400	-19651
New Bank	279087	84.65	1.42	8.34	34.93	41.26	10.41	36.67	9.39	-6761	-7579
PNASB	386897	88.44	2.15	8.53	40.13	45.37	10.28	35.26	9.54	-7086	-19519
Syndicate	995171	89.08	2.02	7.64	42.47	47.68	10.63	30.09	10.23	-10407	-67008
UCO	1248801	80.08	6.59	8.41	46.55	58.12	9.25	27.08	9.28	-11335	-44419
United	733851	83.86	3.88	8.99	39.84	47.51	10.88	35.59	9.09	-12137	-27936
Total	21161356	85.29	4.42	8.27	45.35	53.16	11.75	31.07	10.17	80392	-364891

of SBI Group (28.25%). Out of seven nationalised banks which earns net profit, five banks e.g. Canara Bank, Punjab National Bank, Indian Bank, Union Bank, Oriental Bank etc. have higher percentage of return on investment than the average of 10.17% (Table 2). From Table 3 it can be observed that percentage of income from investment is highest in case of foreign banks (30.25%) and lowest in case of SBI Group (24.83%).

The major source of revenue for commercial banks is from interest on advance. In cases of all the bank groups share of revenue from advances is more than 50% (Table 3). Revenue from advances and investments constitutes more than 76% of total revenue of each Commercial Bank groups (Table 3). Percentage of advance to working fund is highest in case of SBI Group (47.31%) and lowest in case of foreign banks (33.85%) Table 1. Other assets includes office building owned by banks etc.

Table 1 only shows the financial position of commercial banks while Table 2 and Table 3 show performance of the commercial banks with many performance indicators. Out of twenty nationalised banks only eleven banks i.e. 55% of banks earns operating profit and seven banks i.e. 35% of banks earns net profit. So this is a very adverse picture for nationalised banks. From Table 3 it can be observed that except the SBI group and private sector Indian banks, all other four groups of banks incur heavy percentage of losses and among them loss percentage is highest for foreign bank (21.35%). Thus we see overall bank performance is very poor and if improvement measures are not taken, then whole banking sector will collapse in future. In order to overcome the problem of low efficiency Narasimham Committee suggested: (i) functional autonomy and (ii) Standard International Accounting Practices viz. (a) income recognition (b) asset classification (c) provisioning and (d) capital adequacy. To expand credit the bank has been advised to take the following steps in capital front (i) plough back of profit; (ii) fresh equity issue; (iii) debt offering; (iv) revaluation of assets, so that lending capacity of a bank no longer depends upon its surplus funds alone. To strengthen capital base most of the banks are yet to get green signals from the govt. to approach the capital market field. Instead the Govt. has made some budgetary provision to this banks. This actually comes into

TABLE 3

Income and Expenditure of All Scheduled Commercial Banks, 1992-93 on Various Heads for per Rs. 100 earned

	SBI Group	*Nation-alised Banks*	*Public Sector Banks*	*Private Sector Indian Banks*	*Foreign Banks*	*Private Sector Banks*	*Total*
1	2	3	4	5	6	7	8
Income							
Int./Disc. on Adv.	51.87	50.94	51.30	53.03	52.99	53.00	51.54
Income on Investment	24.83	30.23	28.14	25.91	30.25	28.85	28.24
Int. on Bal. with RBI & others	8.63	8.57	8.60	9.64	8.15	8.63	8.60
Other Interest	1.80	0.40	0.94	0.65	0.75	0.72	0.91
(a) Total Interest	87.13	90.14	88.98	89.23	92.14	91.20	89.29
Comm. exch. and Brokerage	9.13	5.36	6.82	6.19	8.55	7.79	6.95
Other Income	3.74	4.50	4.20	4.58	0.69	1.01	3.76
(b) Total other Income	12.87	9.86	11.02	10.77	7.86	8.80	10.71
Total (a+b)	100.00	100.00	100.00	100.00	100.00	100.00	100.00
Expenditure							
Interest	60.28	70.94	66.81	61.52	63.96	63.17	66.30

(Contd.)

TABLE 3 (*Contd.*)

1	2	3	4	5	6	7	8
Establishment Exp.	16.93	17.69	17.39	18.02	5.32	9.41	16.29
Other Current Exp.	5.89	6.80	6.45	6.78	14.03	11.69	7.18
Other non-current Exp.	0.69	0.93	0.84	0.88	1.97	1.62	0.95
Operating Exp.	23.51	25.42	24.68	25.68	21.32	22.72	24.42
Provision & Contingencies	14.06	20.13	17.84	9.76	36.07	27.59	0.19
Profit/Loss	2.15	-16.49	-9.33	3.04	-21.35	-13.48	9.09
Total	100.00	100.00	100.00	100.00	100.00	100.00	100.00

conflicts with the Narasimham Committee recommendation as the govt. steps are mostly based on political consideration.

CONCLUSION

It has been observed that interest spread has largely remained constant over a period of time and cost has increased. It will be difficult for banks to curtail expenditure on manpower as more branches are opened. Expenses for banks also increases due to inflation. So to arrest the declining trend in profitability banks have to introduce suitable costing techniques. A good costing system will help in cost control as also in ascertaining the service cost (i.e. price) below which the customer should not be charged. Thus to sum up the transition of the public sector bank from sort of command economy to a market economy is far from complete. Prior to liberalisation banks had little control over their destiny. However, the new situation offers greater scope for the commercial banks to be an active player in India's capital market.

References

Pujari, N.V., "Asset Liability Management: Some Aspects"; Murali Mohana Krishna, Y., "Business Planning: Some Issues"; Varma, V.K., "Costing and Pricing in Banks: Concept and Philosophy"; Patil, R.H., "Contemporary Banking: Competition and Markets"; *in* Yadav, Narendra (ed): *Challenges to Indian Banking*, Macmillan India Ltd., New Delhi.

RBI (1988), *Report on Currency and Finance 1987-88,* Vol I.

GOI (1989), *Economic Survey 1988-89.*

6

Long-run Behaviour of Indian Money Market: A Spectral Analysis of Call Money Rate

SANJIB CHANDRA BASU AND SUBODH CHANDRA GARAI

The classical macroeconomic framework is highly influenced by the operation of Says' Law which along with Walras' Law leads to determinacy of relative prices. It means a barter economy, i.e., exchange of commodities against commodities. But this type of Walrasian spot transaction may face trouble when time element is introduced in the analysis, i.e., continuous transactions are allowed. Hence there arises a need for Bill Market.

Suppose, bills are accepted as media of payment. But the smooth functioning of the Bill Market may be hampered consequent upon the problem of discounting of bills for (i) difference in reliability of bill issuing authorities; (ii) question of time preference and (iii) the need for reborrowing at the time of repayment, especially in the case of Government. Hence there arises the need for promoting a particular type of firm known as bank and it is entrusted with the development of the transactions like (a) accepting deposits, (b) discounting bills,

(c) making advances to customers and the similar transactions. Now, let us consider a situation where deposits are withdrawable on demand while advances are relatively illiquid, at least partially. Three options are open to meet such a situation:

(1) To take advantage of the law of large numbers;
(2) To maintain sufficient liquidity which is measured by the ratio of reserves to deposits and/or;
(3) To borrow from another bank or similar financial institution, in case of emergency.

Thus the components like currency, demand deposits, treasury bills, trade bills etc. provide a range of options to the economic units in so far as holding of assets is concerned [*Hicks* (1989), Ch. 5 to 7]. The money market is dealing with such short-term instruments. On the other hand, capital market is concerned with long-term instruments like bonds, equities and debentures.

The essential characteristics of a modern and well-developed financial market[1] are:

(1) High-degree of specialisation with regard to dealings in instruments;
(2) Single price for each of the instruments;
(3) Free flow of fund and information from one sub-market to another such sub-market and
(4) Integration of sub-markets.

The present article attempts to analyse the behaviour of call money rate in India. Call money rate is chosen as a money market variable because call money is most frequently resorted to by the money market agencies (e.g., banks) as a very short-term source of finance. Moreover, for a very long period, data on this rate are available, from reliable sources. It is probably the most appropriate short rate which can explain the crucial development in regard to money demand.

STRUCTURAL CHANGES—IMPACT OF POST-LIBERALISED ECONOMY ON CALL MONEY RATE

Market forces, generally, helped to determine call rates in

India till 1973. Following the restrictive credit policy of Reserve Bank of India, call rate rose to an alarming level of 30% p.a. in December, 1973. As a consequence, after several rounds of revisions, the ceiling was placed at 10% p.a. in April, 1980. As an effect of this, the actual behaviour of money market got distorted for a considerable periof of time. Eventually, the Working Group under the chairmanship of Mr. N. Vaghul (following the recommendations of Chakraborty Committee in 1985) suggested the followings:

(1) To widen and deepen the market by relative increase in the number of participants as lenders;

(2) To withdraw the ceiling so that the call rate be determined by market forces of demand and supply and

(3) To equip call money market as a focal point for central bank intervention for influencing liquidity in the economy.

For the implementation of the suggestions of the Working Group, Discount and Finance House of India was established in April, 1988. It was set up to widen the money market operations. Any entity is able to lend in the call money market through DFHI with a minimum size of lending at Rs. 20 crore since April, 1991, provided it has no short-term borrowings from the RBI. Moreover, RBI switched from exorbitantly high graduated penalty system on CRR defaults prevalent till April, 12, 1990 to a more rationalised and downward inclined system of graduated penalty on CRR [*Bhoi*, 1993].

We propose to undertake in this article:

1. Time series analysis of weekly weighted average call money rate for 631 weeks, from 04.01.1985 to 31.01.1997, the data source being various issues of RBI Bulletin.
2. The entire analysis will then be broken into sub-periods, viz.,
   (i) Pre-liberalisation Period—for 339 weeks (04.01.1985 to 28.06.1991) and
   (ii) Post-liberalisation Period—for 201 weeks (02.04.1993 to 31.01.1997).

A similar analysis will also be done on monthly weighted average of call money rate which will be reported in the appendix.

So far as statistical analysis is concerned, the following steps are planned to be followed:

(1) Calculation of periodogram ordinates to identify prominent frequency of sinuosity (periodicity) as well as to identify any time trend;

(2) Fitting the observed data to trend line of

(a) Ordinary polynomial form, viz., of the pth degree for X_t

$$X_t = \sum_{k=0}^{p} a_k t^k + e_t$$: t is in time unit (week/month) and e_t is the residual term,

(b) Grafted polynomial form (being more appropriate due to the ceiling imposed upon the call rate upto the first quarter of 1989);

(3) Calculation of detrend values and computation of periodogram ordinates of this residual series;

(4) Derivation of detrend-desined series and computation of pure residuals;

(5) Comparison of the variance of each of the derived series (of residuals) with the variance of the original series of rate, to measure the efficiency of removal of the influence of trend (as well as the cyclical components) and ascertaining the power retained in the ultimate residuals; and

(6) Comparison of auto-regressive structure of original series and testing of the random walk process, of both the sub-periods.

In this connection, Jenkins and Watts (1968), Koopmans (1974), Brillinger and Krishnaiah (1983), Fuller (1996) and Hidalgo (1996) may be consulted.[2]

(1) Univariate Time Trend and Sinusoidal Pattern

Firstly, let us analyse the time series weekly weighted

average call money rate (Mumbai) for the whole study period, i.e., for 631 weeks starting from the week ended on Friday, the 4th January, 1985 to the week ended on Friday, the 31st January, 1997. The A.M., highest and lowest values of the rate for 631 weeks are respectively 11.858% p.a., 54.5% p.a. and 1.05% p.a. Since the periodogram ordinates at low frequencies are very high, there is a trend in the series. Again, as upto the first quarter of 1989 there was a ceiling limit on call money rate @ 10% p.a. and the rate remained more or less fixed, a grafted linear trend [Fuller (1996), pp. 480-84] is best fitted with the data set (X_t, t=1 for 1st week of 1985) which is

$$X_t = \underset{(28.383)}{10.8871} + \underset{(3.269)}{0.0035}\, z, \text{ here }, z = \begin{cases} t & \text{for } t>224, \\ 0 & \text{otherwise;} \end{cases}$$

F (1,629) = 10.684, t-ratios are given in parentheses with 629 degrees of freedom. Therefore, this finding suggests that the trend was suppressed to be manifested a long period ago. Some periods,[3] corresponding to the frequencies for the sinusoidal pattern of the detrend series for which the periodogram ordinates are significant (at 1% level) as per Kolmogorov-Smirnov-type test [Fuller (1996), pp. 363-66], in order of importance, are—210 weeks, 26 weeks, 63 weeks, 48.5 weeks, 29 weeks, 79 weeks etc., i.e., 4 years, $^1/_2$ years, 1 year $2^1/_2$ months, 11 months, $6^2/_3$ months, $1^1/_2$ years etc.

These periods are also found in the case of the original series (with more or less same level of significance). The variance of the original series is 37.6659. The variances of the detrend and detrend-desined series are respectively 37.0368 and 25.3788. Therefore, 33% of the variance is explained away by trend and sinusoidal influence. Now, to examine whether the results improve, let us consider the two sub-periods within the whole study period, viz., the Pre-liberalisation period and the Post-liberalisation Period. A sub-period, in between these two, being the period of transition with, naturally, no systematic behaviour is avoided for analysis.

Secondly, the above exercise is repeated to analyse the time series of weekly weighted average call money rate (Mumbai) for the Pre-liberalisation Period, viz., for 339 weeks starting from the week ended on Friday, the 4th January, 1985 to the week ended on Friday, the 28th June, 1991. The A.M. of the rate for 339 weeks is 11.753% p.a. and the highest and the lowest values of the rate are 35.44% p.a. and 7.15% p.a. respectively. In this case too, since the periodogram ordinates at low frequencies are of very high values, there is a trend. For the same reason stated in the preceding paragraph, a grafted quadratic trend is best fitted with the data set (X_t, t=1 for 1st week of 1985) which is

$$X_t = \underset{(55.120)}{10.103} + \underset{(20.691)}{0.0011Z^2}, \text{ here, } Z = \begin{cases} t-224 & \text{for } t > 224 \\ 0 & \text{otherwise;} \end{cases}$$

F (1,337) = 428.11, t-ratios are given in parentheses with 337 degrees of freedom.

This improvement of the result is, certainly, giving good grounds for sub-division of the study period into pre-and post-liberalisation periods etc. Some statistically significant (at 1% level as per the test stated earlier) periods of the detrend series for this sub-period, in order of importance, are—

26 weeks, 10 weeks, 15 weeks, 2 weeks, 17 weeks etc., i.e., $^1/_2$ year, $2^1/_3$ months, $3^1/_2$ months, $^1/_2$ month, 4 months etc.

While the same periods are also found in case of the original series for this sub-period (with more or less same level of significance), none but 26 weeks (of these periods) is found in conformity with the periods reported in the foregoing paragraph. For this sub-period, the variances of the original, detrend and detrend-desined series are respectively 20.8387, 9.1787 and 7.0998, that is, about 2/3rd of the total variance has been explained away by the elimination of trend and sinusoidal influence. Obviously, a remarkable degree of improvement is noticed !

Thirdly, the same exercise is again repeated to analyse the time series of weekly weighted average call money rate (Mumbai) for the Post-liberalisation Period, viz., for 201 weeks starting from the week ended on Friday, the 2nd April, 1993 to the week ended on Friday, 31st January, 1997. The A.M., the highest and the lowest values of the rate for 201 weeks are respectively 10.366% p.a., 41.62% p.a. and 1.05% p.a. In this case also, since the periodogram ordinates at low frequencies are of very high values, a trend should exist. A cubic polynominal time trend is best fitted with the data set (X_t, t=1 for the Ist week of April, 1993) which is

$$X_t = 12.1415 - 0.3755t + 0.006\ t^2 - 0.0000219\ t^3;$$
$$(7.775) \quad (-5.624) \quad (7.796) \quad (-8.788)$$

F (3,197) = 40.961, t-ratios are given in parentheses with 197 degrees of freedom.

The trend line is also remarkably different from the corresponding lines reported in the previous two paragraphs, further substantiating the logic behind the sub-division of the total study period. Some significant (at 1% level according to the test mentioned earlier) periods of the detrend series for Post-liberalisation Period, in order of importance, are—

50.25 weeks, 15.50 weeks, 20 weeks, 8 weeks, 12.50 weeks etc., i.e. $11^1/_2$ months, $3^2/_3$ months, $4^1/_2$ months, 2 months, 3 months etc.

For this sub-period also, while almost same periods are found in case of the original series (with more or less same level of significance), none (of these periods) has a counterpart in the two periods already analysed in this sub-section. For this sub-period, the variances of the original, detrend and detrend-desined series are respectively 46.9532, 28.9160 and 14.8790, that is, more than 2/3 rd of the total variance has been explained away by the elimination of trend and sinusoidal influence. Therefore, comparing the results relating to the trend and periodicity pattern, we can validly infer that the behaviour of call money rate in the pre-and post-liberalisation periiods disagrees to a great extent.

In the appendix, results of the analysis of behaviour of the monthly weighted average call money rate (Mumbai) are reported in brief. As division of the whole into the above mentioned sub-periods performed better results, only for the said sub-periods the results are shown.

(2) Comparison of the Auto-regressive Structure and Testing of the Random Walk Process

For the purpose of examination of autoregressive structure, let us analyse the data of the above mentioned two sub-periods for weekly weighted average call money rate (Mumbai). The

AR(1)[4] equations for pre-and post-liberalisation periods respectively are (for the original series)-

$$X_t = \underset{(4.582)}{1.623} + \underset{(30.686)}{0.8645}\, X_{t-1} \text{ with } F\ (1{,}336) = 942 \text{ and}$$

$$X_t = \underset{(3.310)}{1.5582} + \underset{(22.225)}{0.8400}\, X_{t-1} \text{ with } F\ (1{,}198) = 494;$$

t=1 for 2nd week of January, 1985 and of April, 1993 respectively and t-ratios are given in parentheses with 336 and 198 degrees of freedom respectively. Therefore, in Post-liberalisation Period, this relationship has weakened clearly. To test the random walk process, we have to calculate the values of the t-statistic for the said degrees of freedom, corresponding to both the autoregressive equations. But, in these cases, the co-efficients (b's) for X_{t-1} are tested as to whether they are unity or not. That is, in each case, the null hypothesis should be, H_0: b=1. The formula to get the t-ratio is

(b-1)/Standard Error of b.

These t-ratios (absolute values) for the two equations reported in this sub-section are 4.810 and 4.233 respectively. Therefore, at a two tail test, the co-efficients in both the periods are significantly different from unity (at 0.0005 level) and hence the random walk is not supported.

CONCLUSION

This article attempted to analyse the behaviour of call money rate of India for a considerable long period of time covering both pre-and post-liberalisation periods. The results revealed that the behaviour of the call money rate (weekly and monthly weighted average rate of major commercial banks—Mumbai) in two sub-periods mentioned above differs remarkably with respect to the nature of time trend as well as the nature of periodicities in sinusoidal pattern. Again, examination results of autogressive structure showed that an AR(1) process is best fitted with the data albeit in post-liberalisation sub-period such relationship has weakened but the random walk process is not supported, using parametric test on the data of both the sub-periods. The present study is restricted to univariate framework. One may introduce multivariate time series framework incorporating rates on certificates of deposit, commercial paper (middle discount rate), Treasury Bills (cut off yield) etc. This study may also be extended to throw some light on the interaction between money market rates and capital market returns via bivariate coherence (in different frequencies) or bivariate/multivariate causality testing.[5] These extensions will give vent to the real picture of Indian money market components/constituents.

Notes and References

1. About the changing environment of international financial market Ghosh & Ortiz (19940 may be consulted.
2. Algorithms, FORTRAN programs and cited references, for Fourier and spectral (with many other) applications, are available from Press *et. al.* (1992, pp. 530-602).
3. If k be the number of completed periods for a component (orthogonal to other components) sine wave of the series within the study period covered, for n=631 weeks, then Frequency (λ) = k/n, Period (for the sine wave) = n/k and Angular frequency (ω) = 2 $\pi\lambda$.
4. Higher order autoregressive processes do not perform better results in both the two sub-periods.
5. Such types of interaction tests are done by Rama Murthy (1996), Amanulla *et. al.* (1996), Gorai and Basu (Forthcoming) and others.

References

Amanulla, S., Arun Kumar Giri and B. Kamaiah (1996): "Information Arrivals, Stock Price Variability and Market Efficiency in Indian Stock Market", *Artha Vijnana*, Vol. 38, No. 1, March, pp. 20-33.

Bhoi, B.K. (1993); "Analytics of the Recent Call Money Rate Behaviour in India", *Reserve Bank of India Occasional Papers*, Vol. 14, No. 4, pp. 319-34.

Brillinger, D.R. & P.R. Krishnaiah (1983) (ed.), *Time Series in the Frequency Domain*, Handbook of Statistics, Vol. 3, North-Holland, Amsterdam, New York, Oxford.

Fuller, Wayne, A. (1996), *Introduction to Statistical Time Series*, Wiley Series in Probability & Statistics, John Wiley & Sons. Inc., New York, Chichester etc.

Garai, S.C. & S.C. Basu, (Submitted for publication in *Sankhya*, Series B), "Multivariate Causality Testing for Prices in Different Markets: Application of Geweke's Method in Indian Context".

Ghosh, Dilip K. & Edgar Qrtiz (1994) (ed.), *The Changing Environment of Internationall Financial Markets: Issues and Analysis*, St. Martin's Press, New York.

Book reviewed by Rajiv Ranjan, *RBI Occasional Papers*, Vol. 16, No. 2, June, 1995.

Hicks, John (1989); *A Market Theory of Money*, Clarendon Press (Oxford University Press), Oxford.

Hidalgo, J. (1996), "Spectral Analysis for Bivariate Time Series with Long Memory", *Econometric Theory*, Vol. 12, No. 5, pp. 733-92.

Jenkins, Gwilym M. & Donald G. Watts (1968), *Spectral Analysis and its Application*, Holden-Day, Sen Francisco.

Koopmans, L.H. (1974), *The Spectral Analysis of Time Series*, Academic Press, New York and London.

Press, William H., Saul A. Teukolsky, William T. Vetterling & Brian P. Flannery (1992), *Numerical Recipes in Fortran: The Art of Scientific Computing*, Cambridge University Press; First Indian Edn. in 1993 (reprinted in 1996), Foundation Books, New Delhi.

Rama Murthy, Y. Sree (1996), "Stock Prices, Money, Inflation and Real Activity: A Cross-Spectral View", *Artha Vijnana*, Vol. 38, No. 1, March, pp. 34-64.

APPENDIX

Analysis of Pre-liberalisation Period and Post-liberalisation Period Behaviour of Monthly Weighted Average Call Money Rate of Major Commercial Banks—Mumbai.

The behaviour of weekly weighted average call money rate of major commercial banks (Mumbai) is studied and the results of the analyses see reported in a main section of this article. In this appendix the behaviour of corresponding monthly rate is studied comparatively for pre-and post-liberalisation periods.

A grafted polynomial trend (Fuller (1996), pp. 480-84] is found in the case of pre-liberalisation sub-period (for 78 months, January, 1985 to June, 1991) rate. It is worthy of a mention that upto March, 1989 (i.e., for first 51 months) the ceiling of 10% p.a. rate was yet in operation. The trend line for the call money rate, X_t (t=1 for January, 1985 and t=78 for June, 1991) is

$$X_t = \underset{(33.065)}{10.3836} + \underset{(12.0358)}{0.000811}\, Z^3, \text{ here, } z = \{t-51 \text{ for } t > 51, 0 \text{ otherwise};$$

F (1,76) = 144.8594, t-ratios are given in parentheses with 76 degrees of freedom. On the other hand, no such grafted polynomial trend is found in the case of Post-liberalisation Period (for 46 months, April, 1993 to January, 1997) rate. Rather, a cubic polynomial time trend is found for this series, for the said sub-period. The trend line for call money rate, X_t for this sub-period (t=1 for April, 1993 and t=46 for January, 1997) is

$$X_t = \underset{(4.314)}{12.5414} \underset{(-3.250)}{-1.7222} + \underset{(4.466)}{0.1163}\, t^2 - \underset{(-5.014)}{0.0018}\, t^3;\ F(3,42) = 13.785.$$

Here also, t-ratios are given in parentheses with 42 degrees of freedom.

Of the detrend (residual) series, the following periods are found important (arranged accordingly) though using Kolmogorov-Smirnov-type test [Fuller (1996), pp. 363-66] no sinusoidal structure of Post-liberalisation Period rate is found significant (at 5% level):

(1) For Pre-liberalisation Period Rate : 6 months, $6^1/_2$ years, 13 months, $2^1/_3$ months and $3^2/_3$ months;

(2) For Post-liberalisation Period Rate : $11^1/_2$ months, $4^1/_2$ months, $3^1/_2$ months, $2^1/_3$ months and 2 months.

The variances of the monthly weighted average call money rates of the two sub-periods for the original series are 18.4178 and 37.244 respectively. Variances for detrend series are 6.3378 and 18.7658 respectively. Ultimately, more than two-thirds of the variances can be explained away by the removal of trend and sinusoids. In the appended Chart the original series (in brown colour) of monthly call money rate together with the detrend series (in blue colour) of the rate for two sub-periods is depicted. The sub-period, in between the above mentioned two sub-periods, being the period of transition is not considered for analysis at all.

Monthly Weighted Average Call Money Rate (% p.a.) of Major Commercial Banks—Mumbai [Deviation from mean is shown]

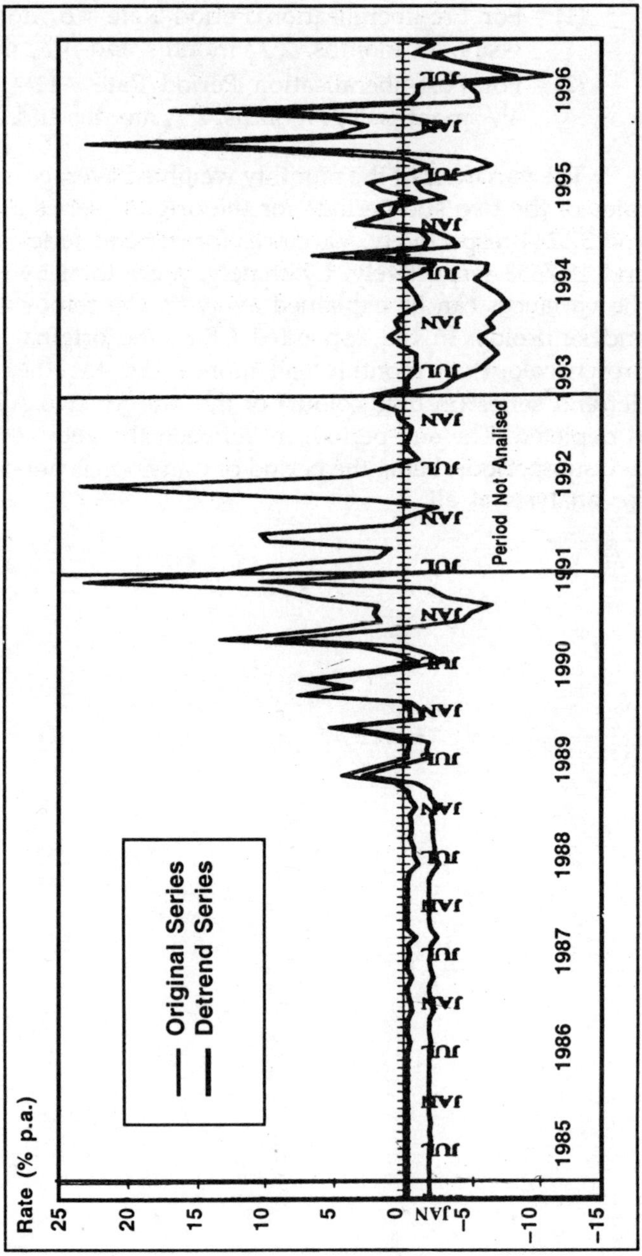

PART C

RURAL MONEY MARKETS

7

Implications of Structural Reforms on Rural Money Market

V.B. JUGALE

INTRODUCTION

The open economy in the early 20th century has a parodoxical experience of crises in 1919 and 1929. The nature of crises was of the extreme situations of overproduction and underproduction. To overcome such odds, controlled economy had been embraced in 1930 onwards. It had been affirmed and strengthened as an effective economic system of integrating all human efforts for the overall betterment of the general public. But during the late 20th century, the controlled economy has failed to attain its goal and lost the credibility of general masses in a few giant controlled economies of the world.

Thatcherism was the humble begining of defending the classical dogma of *laissez faire* in 1970s. The supply side economics in U.S.A. had engendered the prolific plinth of the present economic reforms. The deffenders of the school of thought argued the fact that, functionless capitalism flourished since 40 years under the protection of professed socialist state.

This classical orthodoxy has been acquainted by world's giant organisations viz. IMF and IBRD. It has been designed as a new macro-economic theory with set of interdependent and independent variables. Therefore, it is worth significant to overview the foundation of structural reforms before reviewing its implication on rural money market.

ECONOMICS OF STRUCTURAL ADJUSTMENTS

Structural adjustments are the structural reforms which tend to change the existing structure[1] of the economy. The objectives of change tends to develop the system in a new design. It has a system approach with varieties of structural adjustments beyond the scope of the functional approach. Structural adjustments are circumscribed to sectoral shift from one position to extreme another. Policy has a functional approach with an objective of evaluating its effectiveness within the system framework.

Reforms are the system designs introduced as the long term structural change in the operation and ownership of macro variables. Privatisation in the planned economic system and globalisation in the protectionist regime are the subjective ingredients of the economic reforms.

In 1970s, the IMF had introduced some demand conditionalities as a stabilisation policy[2] for correcting the fiscal inbalances for a short period. On the contrary World Bank was in favour of supply conditionalities[3] and growth conditionalities[4] in the framework of long-term structural changes. Cross conditionalities[5] were also advocated by IMF and IBRD. Now-a-days overall structural changes are termed as reforms in intersectoral and intrasectoral aspects of the body economy.

FINANCIAL SECTOR REFORMS

Financial sector is one of the vast integral part of the body economy directly linked to the process of economic development and co-related and co-existed with goods market and labour market in the economy. It is always stated that, the financial sector (money and finance) has been disdained by economists. The finance has obtained the treatment of the second class citizen.

There is a curve to explore the general theory of finance. The non-banking financial intermediaries have attained a remarkable position in the overall monetary transactions in the economy. Now it is being urged to integrate the views of bankers, NBFI and the monetary theorists for improving the health of the economy.

The financial sector augments to restore the inherent link between producers and consumers. The free flow of funds from one agency to another is more justifiable in the liberalised economy. The financial sector reforms (FSR) is a step towards overall economic reforms. So, the general economic reforms may have certain implications on the financial sector. The FSR are basically consisting of the reforms in (a) Financial system, (b) Financial instruments and operations, (c) Organisational changes in managing the sector. The financial system is normally classified into, (i) Financial institutions, (ii) Financial market and (iii) Financial services. There are varieties of financial instruments used in both money and financial sector.[6]

Financial Liberalisation School (FLS) approach[7] envisages and signifies the free hand to the financial sector, which includes liberalisation of rate of interest, free capital movement, automatic exchange rate adjustment, liberalised credit policy, greater freedom to the banks, free entry to the private sector, reorganisation of the banking system, creating capital base, CAR, autonomy to central banks, privatisation of insurance industry, changes in rating norms and transparency in accounting, establishing bank tribunals to recover loans and to restore monetary discipline in the recommendations of the Narasimham Committee. Normally money supply is the function of business activity and liquidity. Varieties of indegeneous and exogeneous factors influence the money supply and liquidity trend. Inter-sectoral and intra-sectoral market equilibrium can best be established through FLS approach in LDCs. Financial instruments tend to internationalise their scope. Convertibility and free flow of capital has been advocated by the FLS. The salient features of the FSR are:

(i) Real economic development is accompanied by financial development. In actual practice financial development oversees the real output,

(ii) Different forms of NBFI intend to financial deepening and widening in the economy,

(iii) The notion that, the commercial banks normally create the money and NBFI are the brokers of the money has been accepted as fallacious phenomenon,

(iv) Need to reconstruct the monetary policy is warranted. There should be no punishment to the good boys (commercial banks) for the act of the bad boys (NBFI),

(v) The role of government in the FLS approach is a kind of treatment by shock therapy rather than gradual or evolutionary recovery. Sometimes mid-way interaction of the government between two extremes is adovcated.

REFORMS IN OPERATION

The FSRs have their begining in 1950s. The writings of Gurley-Shaw, Sayers, Gustav Schmoiders, Radcliff Committee Report had created the base and background for the FSR. The structural reforms in trade, commerce and industrial activities at the begining of 1990s in India have intensified to bring up the reforms in operation.

The foundation of FSR lies in bestowing ample freedom to the financial sector.[8] Recently the FLS in addition covers the financial efficency norms, financial innovations in capital broadening and capital deepening and capital diversification.

The first and foremost FSR in India has been introduced in credit policy during the year 1991-92. The SLR and CRR have been reduced to attain the limit of Narasimham Committee recommendations (i.e. 25% & 10% respectively). This acceded extra funds to the banks to manage their portfolios.

To increase the capital base of the public sector banks, they have been liberalised to sell part of their share capital in the market. A few banks have initiated with this policy.

The next important reform in the series is deregulation of interest rate ceiling. The interest rates have been fully liberalised to the rural credit and partially it has been made applicable to the rest of the banking sector in the economy. The theory behind removing the artificial ceiling on rate of interest is that, by liberalising the rate of interest, saving, investment and output tend to increase. In the process an inefficient borrowed investment may run away from the market. Only efficient investment (whose marginal efficiency of capital is higher than rate of interest) will survive in the market. Besides quality of investment and allocation of resources improve. During the period of financially repressed regime investment remains self-financed.

The operation and organisation of deregulation of interest rate has actually no worth effects on the macroeconomic variables in India irrespective of its declining changes. The responsibility of fixing the rate of interest is shifted from one agency to another. The rural as well as urban banking units could not arrive at the competent and effective rate of interest of their own. However, the rate of interest tends to decline since last few years, which has direct bearing on increasing investment. The individual financial institutions and individual branches in India could not arrive their own rate of interest as a result of interest rate liberalisation. In fact under the FLS approach rate of interest may remain fluctuating. It is very difficult to arange such affairs to the rural money market, because the rural money market do not possess any expertise. The rural money market is still remained favourable to informal sector. The efforts are being made through reforms to improve the operational efficiency of the overall banking in India.

The rural money market still is facing number of odds in its operation. The loan reoveries of small and marginal farmers in cooperative sector are better than large farmers. Large farmers are habituated to create wilfull defaults. Large farmers have large capacity to borrowing loans. The poor though productive and badly in need of loan assistance do not get sufficient loan amount for their benefit due to their non-creditworthiness. The poors can be made creditworthy through using their productive capacities. The rural areas posses potential possibilities of linking credit to marketing and processing. But the existing credit marketing is impoverish to tackle the challenges of FLS approach.

The branch licensing has been removed. Consequently every banking unit is very cautious about installation of new bank branches. Every banking unit has now started to estimate the break-even levels of their business. This tendency results to centralise the banking industry only in commercially overcrowded areas. The rural credit system has to suffer as a result of this tendency. However, the rural sector has potential capabilities of mobilising the deposits. Besides, now-a-days the economy is becoming more and more segmented. Particularly the manufacturing sector is being decentralised. The non-farm economic activities are being centralised in the rural area. Micro-enterprising is becoming more popular in rural area. Taking this into account the banking sector has potential business in rural area. The productive capacities of the rural masses be identified properly and financial assistance should be made available to them. Creditworthiness of the ruralites can be increased through linking the credit to the marketing and/or processing. The existing system is nothing to do with these potentialities. Of late Self-Help Groups are being linked to the banks. This has challenged the cooperative credit movement. Consequently the overall banking structure and cooperative credit system has to change their operating system. Still there is a strong case for the informal banking system to promote a micro-enterprising business in rural area. They are catalystic agents of financial transactions.

There is a possibility of redefining the priority sector. Narasimham Committee necessitated to change the coverage of priority sector. The non-farm micro-enterprising units and small-scale instrustries including village industries are tending to centralise in rural atmosphere. The rural infrastructural development has now became the fundamental activity of the government. As a result the internal and external economies are being created in rural area. The micro-enterprising and SSI units have a great scope in rural area. The Second Census of SSI, has indicated the fact that, 96% of industrial units are SSI units and micro-enterprising units. Whose share in output is 55% with 70% share in employment and the range of investment is above Rs. 50,000 each. Nayak Committee (1992) has rightly pointed out the significance of increasing their working capital and making it convenient to assist to the SSI and village industries. Now-a-days the small loans are most profitable. Bank Rokyat Indonesia has proved this. Even in India also S.T. loans by commercial banks are declining, whereas term loans are increasing. Similarly loans to agriculture sector is declining whereas loans to allied activities are increasing. This is rather a good symptom.

Banking units are now focusing their attention on three principles, viz. efficiency, productivity and profitability. Operational flexibility is on the card. Whereas functional autonomy yet to come.

Lot of changes are taking place in financial instruments. The technological innovations are rewarding both to the bankers and to the customers. In near future actual money will be used less due to such innovation. Internet and INSAT technology has created lot of potentialities in bringing out the banking industry in a forefront.

IMPLICATIONS OF REFORMS ON RURAL MONEY MARKET

Conceptually rural money market (RMM) consists of agencies of all types dealing with collection of deposists and practicing credit business in rural area. Now-a-days rural capital market is also growing gradually. Rural area normally has two types of activities viz. Farm and Non-Farm. As said earlier recently all types and all sizes of industrial activities are localising with their complementary tertiary sector in rural area. RMM in India has different characteristics and requires different treatments and considerations as compared to urban money market. RMM is actually a credit marketing market. Mobilisation of deposits from rural area has been discarded by the credit institutions. Even cooperatives also failed to mobilise the resources from rural area.

The Narasimham Committee has not covered the cooperative sector in its recommendations. This is the serious flaw left in the Report. Cooperative sector is an integral part of financial system in India. The sector has vital share in agricultural business. (Table 1) However, the sector may have direct and indirect effects of the reforms.

The share of investment in rural sector will increase in near future, because of the centralisation of non-farm activities in rura area. The financial institutions (private and public) are more interested in financing these activities. This alarming growth may have adverse consequences on farm activities like reluctancy in delivering farm credit particulary to foodgrains production. Investment in farm activities may face adversity.

TABLE 1

Percentage of Agricultural Borrowing from different Agencies

Agencies	*AIRCS 1951*	*AIRDIS 1961*	*NCAER 1971*	*NSS 37 Round*
Government	3.3	2.3	3.6	4.5
Cooperatives	3.1	15.5	22.7	28.7
Commercial Banks	0.9	0.6	4.0	28.0
Money Lenders	75.0	58.0	49.6	20.2
Friends/Relatives	14.2	8.8	18.9	18.6
Land Lords	3.3	8.8	1.3	—

Source: Theories of Agricultural Finance—V.B. Jugale, Atlantic Publishers & Distributors, New Delhi, 1991.

Production credit may not be supplied by the credit agencies if the condition of priority lending is removed. NFS in rural area is generating employment opportunities. Consequently migration towards urban area will be reduced. Trading and commercial activities in rural area will increase phenomenally.

The agriculture sector has regular demands of credit for production purposes. There is a minor growth in its performance as compared to financing to the NFS. The rate of capital formation in agriculture sector is deteriorating since last 20 years. The existing technology in agriculture sector may not intend to generate employment opportunities further. So, the dependency on agriculture will be reduced further to 55% by the end of 2000 A.D. The subsidiary activities to agriculture sector in rural area will gear up their growth rate at the satisfactory level.

The concept of priority sector lending will change as a result of Narasimham Committee recommendations. The investment of commercial banks in NABARD bonds is being considered as priority sector lending. The role and responsibilities of NABARD will significantly go up as an apex body in agricultural financing. A step to increase the capital base of NABARD has been taken up as an important feature of the budget for the year 1997-98.

Large-scale agri-business will take place in near future as a result of economic reforms. Agricultural exports will increase. This will intend to reorient the rural credit market. Agri-business normally places its attention on the commercial crops. As a result, production of food crops will decline. The credit agencies in fact are not interested to lend for agricultural production. Therefore, there is a possibility of change in organisation and operations of the rural credit market immediately after the withdrawal of state support.

The domination of unorganised agencies in supplying credit to both rural and urban sector has yet not been minimised. Its domination in urban area is increasing. Small businessmen, industrial workers and non-creditworthy self-employed persons are more dependent on unorganised agencies. There is a phenomenal growth of credit societies both in rural and urban areas, since they give easy loans to its members. This has an adverse impact on the business of commercial banks. The organised financial market except urban banks in the present context is unable to fetch the overall credit needs. This will create a background for having private banks in rural credit dealings. Regional rural private banks is in the agenda of reform.

Restructurisation of the cooperative credit system will be the next step towards phenomenal reforms in the financial sector. NABARD is also in favour of restructurisation of cooperative credit system. Recently NABARD has advised the Maharashtra Government to initiate in reorganisation of PACS. The responsibilities of grass root level agencies in cooperative credit structure will bring new vistas and challenges. Therefore, reforms is a challenge and an opportunity to the cooperative sector.

The private sector has a great scope in rural credit market. The rural sector has an ample potential of mobilising resources. The existing banking system is unable to harness the small savings potentials from rural area. The small marketable surpluses are neglected. The cooperatives are also unable to mobilise the saving resources. The disguised saving potentials is in fact the real inspiration of the growth, because greater the backwardness, greater are the possibilities of development. Proper channelisation of resources with the capability of recycling the resource is strictly required for deepening and widening of the rural money market in India.

Rural credit policy and supervision on credit agencies also deserve reorganisation of the banking system. Narasimham Committee suggested the ways and means to supervise and to bring transparency in bank accounting. Financial liberalisation necessitated the RBI, SEBI and other government organisations to supervise over the financial institutions. Supervision has now become an inevitable function of these agencies so as to create credibility among the investors and depositors which is a must. Liberalisation ought not be considered as full freedom. The freedom itself is regulated one. The significance of NBFI in financial sector is growing. As a result there is a need to cover these agencies under the credit and monetary policy of the central banks. Otherwise commercial banks will unnecessarily and indirectly punished. The overall circular flow of funds towards NBFI is growing. They are creating great deal of enthusiasm in activating the deposits and investments even in rural area.

An effective alternative to cooperatives are the NGOs and SHGs. Of late these institutions have attained a great deal of favouritism in rural sector. The financial institutions are also more enthusiastic in lending for the betterment of the homogeneous small group of the rural society. This will significantly minimise the importance of cooperative credit institutions in rural area. The NFS activitiess simultaneously will make their seperate places of significance in the rural area. The existing cooperative system, if not restructured will only perform the traditional regulated credit delivery functions for the benefit of the landholders through financing for crop cultivation. Commercial crop, horticultural crops and oilseed crops have a great scope to receive credit facilities. As a result there will be a change in the cropping pattern.

Trade liberalisation as said earlier is a challenge and an opportunity to the agricultural sector. Agricultural export dealings in the new area of international trading business, the pre-harvest and post-harvest agricultural technology may become more scientific and market oriented. The financing for such dealings will be the new avenues to the credit market.

As an outcome of structural reforms, delicensing and decontrol of agro-industries may create some prominent problems. Organisation and operating of agro-industries under cooperative principles is more rewarding to the agriculturists. The entry of private sector as a result of reforms will spoil the interests of the agricuturists. Exploitation of the farmers may persist due to privatisation of agro-industries.

Any credit system should not make the farmers indebted; on the contrary it should reorient to develop the farm families. Today every farm family is indebted. They manipulate to repay the loans by renewing the loan proposals. The credit agencies are also in favour of such transactions. The credit market today is the lenders market. The institutional lenders always try to remain safe by managing the port-folios. The non-institutional agencies partially care for their safeness in lending even to the non-creditworthy borrowers, so, the popularity of such agencies is still existing. The entry of private sector credit agencies in the rural money market may create the problem of indebtedness. Consequently the background for riots like Deccan riot in 1875s may get generated. So, there is need to supervise the rural credit market by instituting a separate statutory supervisory organisation. Government do not reject its socio-economic obligations towards the welfare of the masses. Administration and supervision should have to be made more effective and public oriented rather than creating the bureaucratic obstructions in the process. The FSRs tends to reorgnise the cooperative sector so as to reorient the agricultural finance with dynamism in its traditional operations. The proper legislative steps should be taken as a policy decision to restructure the system. As a result of liberalisation, government will withdraw its share capital. Consequently the cooperatives have to establish their resource base. (In fact government capital in cooperatives is very small as compared to private sector. Even though government interference is great in cooperatives as compared to private sector.) The Cooperatives should be reoriented towards member driven, member control and member responsive organisations.

In conclusion it can be stated that, the structural reforms

in general and financial sector reform in particular is a challenge as well as an opportunity to the rural credit market. The challenges can be faced only by reorganising and reorienting the rural credit market. In fact rural sector has a disguised potentials of credit business. So one has to identify them and try to harness the benefits. Making the people more productive by linking credit to marketing and processing is a safest procedure to both the parties. Even a non-creditworthy people can also be included in this system. The NFS has ample scope in rural area to establish its significance further. Not only this but the NFS has potential capability also to generate employment opportunities in rural sector. Structural reforms though advocate liberalisation and more openness is a regulated plan strategy of the national authority.

Notes and References

1. The structure had been defined by Alfred Marshall. (1920) as "..................... is used to distinguish in relation to their contribution to GDP between the primary sector of the economy, secondary sector and the tertiary sector————————". According to I.M.D. Little (1950). "Structure is used to democrate and distinguish between those areas of the economy where the state intervention and direction is predominant as against those areas of the economy which are left mainly to the free play of market forces." In the Indian context the economic structure is described as being a mixed economy with the infrastructures, large scale industries and banking and credit institutions being owned and managed by government of the state and agriculture, fishing, animal husbandary, minor irrigation and medium and small industries being owned and run by individuals in accordance with market forces with some government controls.
2. (a) Cutting government expenditure, (b) Currency devaluation, (c) Raising rate of interest and (d) Trade liberalisation.
3. (a) Project formulation and implementation, (b) Structural adjustment lending, (c) Investment programmes, (d) System of incentives, (e) Pricing (f) Financial liberalisation, (g) Trade liberalisation.
4. (a) Free hand and incentives to private sector (b) Privatisation of government owned enterprises (c) Promotion of foreign direct investment, (d) Trade liberalisation.
5. (a) Reduction of deficits and control on inflation, (b) Subsidy programmes be eliminated, (c) Elimination of expenses on social welfare, (d) Limitations on wage hike, (e) Encourage foreign investment, (f) Improve competitive efficiency.
6. Bhole, L.M. (1992), Financial Institutions and Market : Structure,

Growth and Innovation. Tata MacGraw Hill Pub., New Delhi.
7. *Indian Economic Journal*, Vol. 39, No. 1 July-Sept. 1991.

References

Marshall, Alfred (1920): Industry and Trade in Principles of Economics.
Little, I.M.D. (1950), A Critique of Welfare Economics.
Das, Debendra (1988), Structural Adjustment in India, Vol. I & Vol. II, Deep & Deep Publications, New Delhi.
Sau, R. (1992), Model of Structural Adjustment through Classical Model, *Economic Times*, Vol. 32 No. 87.
E.P.W., Vol. XXXII, No. 23, 1-6 June 1997.

8

Nature and Extent of Interlinkage of Agrarian Credit Markets: A Case of Punjab

GIAN KAUR AND ANITA GILL

Rural credit markets in India have been at the centre of policy intervention. Initial step towards this direction goes as back as 1904 when the co-operative movement was launched and subsequently co-operative banks were directed to extend credit to the agricultural sector. Nationalisataion of 14 major commercial banks in 1969 and another 8 banks in 1980 was a landmark in institutionalising rural credit. These banks were asked to direct 17 percent to 18 percent of their total lending to the agriculture sector. In 1975, Regional Rural Banks (RRBs) were set up to strengthen the institutional rural credit market. Quantitatively the contribution of these institutions to rural credit market has increased over time and it is as targeted.

A special feature of the Indian rural credit market is the co-existance of the formal and informal sectors. Formal sector includes the financial institutions regulated by the government, whereas the Informal credit sector comprises of professional money-lenders, relatives and friends, traders and landlords.

Terms and conditions of credit contracts among these two sources are known to be markedly different, ranging from cheap, subsidized institutional loans with collateral requirements, to usurious loans with or without collateral from the private money lenders.

The decennial surveys, initiated in 1951, on rural debt reveal a steady growth of lending by financial institutions to rural households. While 80 percent of all rural debt was owed to the money lenders in 1951, it was mere 24 percent in 1981. The official estimates were challenged by two independent surveys of particular areas of India. The first was World Bank research project covering villages from the states of Andhra Pradesh, Bihar and Punjab. Another covered the villages of the states of Andhra Pradesh, Madhya Pradesh and Maharashtra by Bell (1990). The surveys observed that the aggregate real debt of cultivators in 1981 was two to five times greater than the official estimates. And the money-lender, though has lost ground relative to institutions over the period 1951-81, he remained an important source of finance to rural households and his volume of business grew.

Several other studies—Ghate (1992), Swaminathan (1991), Sarap (1990), Bell and Srinivasan (1987), Sarap (1987) have reaffirmed the presence and importance of the informal sector in rural credit market over and above the formal sector. The informal sector is characterized by highly personalized loan transactions entailing face to face dealings with borrowers and flexibility in respect of loan amount, purpose, interest rate, collateral requirements, maturity period etc. At the other end is the formal sector where the scale of operations is much larger, but transactions are not done face to face, and loan terms regarding amount, purpose, interest rate etc. are standardized. Internal bureaucratic procedures usually raise transaction costs in the formal sector to levels much above that in the informal sector.

Informal credit market has thus retained its existance in the rural credit market. Moneylender in this market is found to be engaged in other activities as well like agriculture, trade etc. As found in the present study, moneylender is the landlord who finances his labour engaged on his land; he is a trader who finances the farmer subject to the condition that he will sell his crop to the trader or he is an input dealer who lends money with undertaking that inputs for cultivation will be purchased only from him. All this gives rise to transactions carried out between the lender and the borrower. These are termed as interlinked credit transactions.

INTERLINKAGES IN THE CREDIT MARKETS

Interlinked credit contracts are finalised face-to-face by the lender and the borrower. Interlinkage is beneficial both to the lender as well as the borrower. In case of landlord/lender and the labourer/borrower, landlord lends with the assurance of labour supply during peak period and the labourer in return gets loan easily by offering his labour service and securing his job throughout the year. In case of a trader lender, he lends to the farmer with the pledge of future selling of his crop. The borrower gets rid of worrying about storage and finding buyer for his output. The trader has the incentive to get interest on the loan, commission on the buying and selling of the product of the farmer/borrower. In addition he may force the farmer to buy inputs like pesticides and fertilizers from him, sometimes at higher prices with poor quality. The process of interlinked transactions involve both the lenders and the borrowers. According to Bell and Srinivasan (1989, 73), 'An interlinked transaction is one in which the parties trade in at least who markets on the condition that the terms of all traders between them are jointly determined'.

A few empirical investigations on the issue of interlinkages involving rural credit have appeared in case of India. Mention may be made of studies by Darling (1925), Bardhan and Rudra (1978) for the states of West Bengal, Bihar and U.P. in 1975-76, Bliss and Stern (1982) followed by Dreze and Mukherjee (1987) for the same village (Palampur), Sarap (1986) in Western Orissa, Kutty (1988) supplemented Sarap's work and analyzed interlinked transactions in Kerala in case of coconut growers. Bell and Srinivasan (1989) did such survey in case of the states of Andhra Pradesh, Bihar and Punjab. Such studies are also noted in case of other countries like Wharton (1962) in Malaya, Jones (1980) for Ghana, Aleem (1990) for Pakistan, Siamwalla *et. al.* (1990) of Thai rural credit market, Floro and Yotopoulos (1991) surveyed fourteen villages in Phillipine Collier and Lal (1985) find no evidence of interlinkage involving credit in Kenya.

The interlinked contracts, though mutual between the lender and the borrower are not in favour of the borrower. The studies mentioned here conclude that such contracts exploit the borrowers. The lenders in the informal credit market enjoys a position of monopoly and are successful in charging exorbitant rates of interest—two to five times the rate charged in the formal credit sector. There is usually implicit rate of interest. In labour-linked transactional, labour is assured of his services at wages much less than market wage rate or he is required to spend more hours in the field.

The main focus of the study is (i) to identify the nature and extent of interlinkage in the informal credit market of the study region and (ii) to identify and analyse the determinants of interlinked contracts.

Data used in this study are based on the investigations carried out in Patiala—one of the seventeen districts of the State of Punjab. Out of the nine blocks of the district, three blocks, Patiala, Ghanaur and Samana—were chosen at random. The villages in each of these blocks were divided into developed and less-developed on the basis of productivity, for which statistics from the Agriculture Department, Punjab, were made use of. Two villages—one developed and one less-developed were selected from each block under consideration and thus in all six villages were surveyed.

Around 40 cultivators and landless labourers were chosen from each village. Due to non-response of some households, the sample size finally turned out to be 181 of which 29 were landless labourers and 152 were cultivators, ranging from marginal farmers (owning land upto 2.5 acres) to extra-large farmers (owning more than 25 acres of land). Information for one agricultural year 1993-94 was collected to cover two crop seasons and effort was made to capture sufficiently the intricacies of interlinked transactions. The information was collected through personal interview with the help of a detailed questionnaire.

Marginal and small farmers (with area upto 5 acres)

together constituted 42 percent of the households and owned about 14 percent of the area. This group has 17 percent of the total operated area, as these farmers have also leased in land. As mechanisation is a common feature in all these villages (in fact in all the villages of Punjab), this group of farmers have no bullock power to till the land, they hire tractor from the medium and larger farmers. The market for hiring tractors is quite developed in the countryside. All the villages have a well developed system for irrigation and water for irrigation was available to small and marginal farmers without installing tubewells and pumpsets themselves which has further reduced costs for marginal and small farmers.

Medium and large sized farmers (with land holding of 5–25 acres) constituted 51.97 percent of the households and occupied 67.11 percent of the area owned. They had larger shre of leased in land (64.25 percent), which shows a clear case of reverse tenancy. Since more of the tenancy contracts are oral and informal in nature, the access to credit from the formal sources of finance on this basis is not available at all. Wheat and paddy are two main crops in all the villages surveyed.

Among the six villages surveyed Soghalpur is the only one which does not have a co-operative society in the village. Table 1 shows the number of households borrowings from different sources according to size of operational holdings.

As is evident from Table 1, the maximum number of households borrowed from the private sources. From the formal sources, the co-operatives contributed more than other formal agencies. The reasons explained were the cumbersome process involved in getting a loan from such agencies and the demand for a collateral (mainly land) by these agencies. To top it all, commercial banks charge a compounding rate of interest on credit, which makes it relatively costly. Among the various categories of holdings, while the medium and larger farmers have made use of both the formal and informal sources of credit to more or less the same extent. Marginal farmers and landless labourers have borrowed more from the private sources. This is because private sources do not usually ask for a fixed asset as collateral, and loan is readily available as and when demanded.

TABLE 1

Number of Households Borrowing from different Sources according to size of Operational Holdings

Size Group of (Holding (Acres)	*Co-operatives/ Land Development*	*Commercial Banks and All other Development Banks*	*All Private Agencies*	*Not Borrowed from any Source*	*Total*
Landless	5 (15.63)	3 (9.37)	18 (56.25)	6 (18.75)	32 (100)
Upto 2.5	13 (31.71)	6 (14.63)	21 (51.22)	1 (2.44)	41 (100)
2.5–5	24 (41.38)	4 (6.90)	27 (46.55)	3 (5.17)	58 (100)
5–10	29 (39.19)	6 (8.11)	36 (48.65)	3 (4.05)	74 (100)
10–25	27 (35.53)	16 (21.05)	33 (43.42)	—	76 (100)
Above 25	15 (32.61)	9 (19.56)	22 (47.83)	—	46 (100)

Source: Field Survey.

Notes: 1. Figures in parentheses are percentage.

2. '—' implies Nil.

TABLE 2

Number of Households Involved in various Types of Interlinked Credit Transactions in the Informal Credit Market

Size of owned holding (acres)	*No. of house-holds*	*Source of borrowing*	*Types of Linkages with*						*Mode of leading*	*Mode of repayment*	*Not borrowed from informal source*
			Land	Labour	Input	Output	Both input and output	None			
Landless	29	Landlords, C.A., Cloth Merchant	—	17	—	2	1	1	Cash, Grain, Input	Labour, Crop	8
Upto 2.5	25	C.A. landlord	—	1	—	16	5	1	Cash, input	Crop, Cash, Labour	2
2.5-5	39	C.A. landlord	—	—	—	25	5	2	Cash, Input	Crop, Cash	7
5-10	41	C.A. landlord	1	—	—	32	3	1	Cash, Input	Crop, Cash	4

10-25	38	C.A.	1	—	—	35	1	—	Cash, Input	Crop and Mortgage	2
Above 25	9	C.A.	—	—	—	8	—	—	Cash	Crop	1
Total	181		2 (1.10)	18 (9.95)	—	118 (65.19)	15 (8.29)		5 (2.76)		24

Source: Field survey.
Notes: 1. (—) Implies Nil.
2. Figures in parenthesis are percentage.
3. C.A. implies commission agent.

The main focus of the study is on informal credit and the interlinkages invoved in such credit deals. Table 2 shows the main sources of informal credit for the different classes of sample households and the different types of linkages thereof.

As evident from the table, the commission agent/trader or *'arhtiyas'* as they are commonly called in Punjab, are the most dominant source of informal credit in the study region for reasons already explained. In our sample, 118 households (65.19 percent) borrowed on the basis of crop as a collateral alongwith the condition of buying farm inputs by the borrower from the trader. This signifies linkage of credit with input as well as output. The rate of interest charged by these lenders was found to be between 24 percent and 36 percent.

Table 3 shows the different categories of households borrowing with linked and non-linked credit transactions for the sample households. Column 3 of the table shows that the majority of borrowers (83.98 percent) obtained credit through linked transactions. And the percentage of borrowers in this category more or less increased with the size of holding. This result is in sharp contrast to the study by Sarap (1991) where the proportion of linked borrowers is higher among the landless households and generally falls with an increase in the size of holding. Linked transactions in the present case were the highest among large and extra large farmers (94.74 and 88.89 percent respectively). The reason behind this can be traced back to the advent of green revolution in the state. Extensive mechanisation in agriculture asks for increased inputs of higher quality and hence enhanced demand for credit of easy access i.e. informal credit. This is confirmed by the fact that a greater share of such expenses (35.27 percent) was met by the informal sector as against only 4.79 percent by formal sector for the sample households.

Table 4 presents the different categories of interlinked transactions, and the percentage of households involved in these transactions both for developed and less developed villages. In both the cases, as given in the table, the most common type of linked transaction that the borrowers are involved in is the credit output linkage. In the developed villages, trying to credit with both input and output that followed the credit-output linked transactions (14.74 percent). Transactions involving land

TABLE 3

Extent of Interlinked Transactions in the Informal Credit Market

Size of owned holding (acres)	*No. of households in the group*	*No. of borrowers with interlinked transactions*	*No. of borrowers with non-linked transactions*	*No. of interlinked borrowers getting formal loan also*	*No. of non-linked borrowers getting formal loans also*	*No. of borrowers borrowing ony from formal source*	*Non-borrowers from any source*
(1)	(2)	(3)	(4)	(5)	(6)	(7)	(8)
Landless	29	20 (68.97)	1 (3.45)	7 (35)	—	2	6
Upto 2.5	25	22 (88.00)	1 (4.00)	17 (77.27)	—	1	1
2.5–5	39	30 (76.92)	2 (5.13)	26 (86.67)	2	4	3
5–10	41	36 (87.80)	1 (2.44)	28 (77.78)	1	1	3
10–25	38	36 (94.74)	—	28 (77.78)	1	2	—
Above 25	9	8 (88.89)	—	6 (75.00)	—	1	—
Total	181	152 (83.98)	5 (2.76)	112 (73.68)	3	11	13

Source: Field Survey.

Notes:

1. Figures in parentheses are percentage of the figure given in column 2.
2. Figures in parentheses in column 5 are percentage of figures given in column 3.
3. '—' implies nil.

TABLE 4

Percentage of Household Involved in different Types of Credit Transactions in the Developed and Less Developed Villages

Size of owned Holdings	Developed Villages							Less Developed Villages						
	No. of house-holds in the groups	Type of Credit Linkage with						No. of house-holds in the groups	Type of credit Linkages with					
		Land	Labour	Input	Output	Both Input and Output	None		Land	Labour	Input	Output	Both	None input and output
Landless	16	—	56.25	—	6.25	—	—	13	—	61.54	—	7.69	7.69	7.69
Upto 2.5	8	—	12.50	—	87.50	—	—	17	—	—	—	52.94	29.41	5.88
2.5–5	15	—	—	—	66.67	—	13.33	24	—	—	—	62.50	20.83	—
5–10	21	—	—	—	90.48	—	—	20	5.00	—	—	65.00	15.00	5.00
10–25	21	—	—	—	85.71	4.76	—	17	5.88*	—	—	100.0	—	—
Above 25	5	—	—	—	80.00	—	—	4	—	—	—	100.00	—	—
Total	86	—	11.63	—	68.60	1.16	2.33	95	2.10	8.42	—	62.10	14.74	3.16

Source: Field Survey.

Notes: 1. *implies that the percentage adds upto more than 100 as there was multiple linkage in case of one borrower, who had borrowed on crop as well as by mortgaging part of his land.

2. '—' implies Nil.

linked with credit were completely absent in the developed villages, but existed marginally (2.1 percent) in the less developed villages.

EMPIRICAL RESULTS

Having established the extent and types of interlinked credit transactions, the study aims at identifying specific characteristics of the sample households, which could possibly play a role in their decision to go in for such transactions. For this purpose Binomial Profit Model has been estimated by the maximum likelihood method. Estimation is done for (i) Land-owning and landless households and (ii) for developed and less developed villages separately. The dependent variable is linked credit transaction. The dummy dependent variable is 1 if the household is linked, O otherwise.

The independent variables include:

Area owned (X_1)

Higher owned area, higher excess to formal sector is expected as land serves to be a good collateral for the institutional loan and hence a negative relation between land owned and linked credit transactions is expected. But as discussed in the previous section high mechanisation of agriculture in the study area may lead to increased demand for informal credit and so positive relation is expected in this case.

Share of leased-in land in the total operated Area (X_2)

Because ownership of land does not increase in this case (in many cases leased-in is oral/informal and not official), but commercialisation of agriculture of the sample are asks for funds, which could be met from the informal sector only (land as collateral is not asked for). Therefore greater is X_2, greater will be the linkages and hence positive sign is expected.

Caste (X_3)

Lower caste households may be discriminated as against their counterparts in borrowing from informal sources. Lower caste is likely to have lower linkage and this may change in case the borrower owns sufficient land.

Education (X_4: X_5, X_6, X_7)

Formal education will have a negative relation with linked credit transactions. As higher the formal education, more aware is the borrower to get formal loan. For econometric analysis variable X_4 is further categorised into primary education (X_5), secondary education (X_6) and higher (matric and above) education (X_7). So higher the education, lower linked transactions are expected.

Proportion of Adult Earning Members (X_3)

Adults engaged in agriculture and increasing income will increase linkage. If engaged in non-agricultural activities, their income adds to the agriculture income and they demand less credit and hence negative relation in linkage is expected. Variable (X_9) is introduced to cover non-agricultural occupation of households.

Productivity (X_{10})

More productivity means more income and less demand for funds, resulting in negative association with linked transactions.

Proportion of Non-Crop Income in total Income (X_{11})

Income in this case, constitutes wage income, salary from jobs outside agriculture. This variable is expected to be negatively associated with linked transactions.

Per Capita Debt (X_{12})

Indebtedness places a household in a weak bargaining position. Hence indebtedness is positively by associated with linkages.

Ownership of Agricultural Assets (X_{13})

More ownership of these assets, higher may be indebtedness of the owners and hence this variable is expected to be positively associated with linked transactions.

Maximum likelihood estimations of Binomial Probit Model have been presented in Table 5 and Table 6. Table 5 shows the estimation separately for the land-owning and landless

TABLE 5
Maximum Likelihood Estimation of Binomial Probit Model (at Household Level)

Variation	*Land Owning Households Coefficients*		*Landless Households Coefficients*
	A	B	
X_1	-0.022161 (-0.926)	-0.022045 (-0.0907)	—
X_2	0.70264 (0.789)	0.92946 (1.001)	—
X_3	0.51889*** (1.613)	0.60131 (1.783)	2.8241 (0.065)
X_4	-0.06921 (-0.219)	—	-1.4477 (-1.006)
X_5	—	0.58119 (0.833)	—
X_6	—	-0.44726 (-1.050)	—
X_7	—	0.64461 (0.144)	—
X_8	1.2712 (1.129)	1.1713 (1.018)	-0.35885 (0.219)
X_9	0.07836 (0.0225)	0.25425 (0.673)	-0.5516 (-0.731)
X_{10}	-0.018794 (-0.491)	-0.015874 (-0.409)	—
X_{11}	-2.1783* (-2.524)	-2.3455* (-2.648)	—
X_{12}	0.021572 (0.914)	0.21704 (0.885)	1.9327** (2.118)
X_{13}	0.15739 (0.965)	0.1365 (0.806)	—
Constant	0.81889 (1.239)	0.72380 (1.087)	-0.12812 (-0.142)
No. of observations	152	152	29

Note: In Category A, education (X_4) has been taken at aggregate level, while in category B, education has been subdivided into primary (X_5), upto secondary (X_6), and matric and above (X_7).

2. *The coefficient is significant at 1 percent level.

** The coefficient is significant at 5 percent level.

*** The coefficient is significant at 10 percent level.

3. Figures in parentheses are t-ratios.

4. '–' implies variables not investigated.

households. The land-owning households have been considered twice in the table, first by considering education on an aggregate

TABLE 6

Maximum Likelihood Estimation of Binomial Probit Model (for land owning households of developed and less-developed villages)

Variable	*Developed Villages Coefficients*		*Less-Developed Villages Coefficients*	
X_1	-0.052735	-0.47551	-0.030116	-0.15551
	(-1.097)	(-0.971)	(-0.440)	(-1.504)
X_2	32.105	29.156	-2.3761	-2.7768
	(0.115)	(0.108)	(1.297)	(-1.375)
X_3	-0.32287	-0.21729	1.874*	2.7786*
	(-0.447)	(-0.285)	(2.455)	(2.645)
X_4	1.2688**	—	0.33441	—
	(1.620)		(-0.553)	
X_5	—	1.7941	—	5.6918
		(0.671)		(0.128)
X_6	—	0.35576	—	-1.2414
		(0.246)		(-1.463)
X_7	—	1.4610***	—	-0.28514
		(1.702)		(-0.235)
X_8	-0.89460	-1.0562	4.0457	3.3344
	(-0.391)	(-0.418)	(1.472)	(1.096)
X_9	-0.81918	-0.48055	1.0632	1.7687*
	(-0.799)	(-0.418)	(1.378)	(1.684)
X_{10}	0.20335	0.19907	-0.05831	-0.056083
	(1.464)	(1.436)	(-0.730)	(-0.696)
X_{11}	-3.9062	-4.2027	-3.0416**	-3.3579***
	(1.343)	(-1.392)	(1.749)	(1.758)
X_{12}	1.0484**	1.0783**	-0.033287	-0.042045
	(1.978)	(1.938)	(-1.217)	(-1.358)
X_{13}	0.090452	0.0099531	1.2422**	1.9448*
		(0.023)	(2.014)	(2.382)
Constant	-0.48733	-0.85416	-1.0061	-1.6126
	(-0.287)	(-0.485)	(-0.725)	(-1.047)
No. of observations	70	70	82	82

Note: In Category A, education (X_4) has been taken at aggregate level, while in category B, education has been subdivided into primary (X_5), upto secondary (X_6), and matric and above (X_7).

2 * The coefficient is significant at 1 percent level.

** The coefficient is significant at 5 percent level.

*** The coefficient is significant at 10 percent level.

3. Figures in parentheses are t-ratios.

level (A), and then by considering categories of education (B). This was not done for the landless class, as a majority of them were completely illiterate, only a few had studied upto the primary level.

The regression coefficients of all the variables expect for X_8 (for both groups), and X_9 (in land-owning households only) have the expected sign. Also X_5 and X_7 do not bear the expected sign. However none of these variables is statistically significant. The variables with expected sign and with statistical significance are the caste (X_3) and proportion of non-crop income in total income (X_{11}) in case of land owning classes, and per capita debt (X_{12}) in case of landless households. Thus, caste, proportion of non-crop income in total income and per capita debt turn out to be the variable which significantly influence the household's decision to go in for linked transactions.

Table 6 presents the similar results for the sample households as belonging to the developed and the less developed villages (classified on the basis of agricultural productivity). Here only land-owning house holds have been taken into consideration.

In case of developed villages, caste (X_3) have the negative sign because in this case an entire village (Ramgarh) of the three developed villages consisted of lower caste but landowning households. As already explained caste variable plays its role subject to the level of land ownership. However, this variable bearing negative sign turned out to statistically non-significant. Productivity (X_{10}) bears positive sign, though statistically non-significant. It may be because of the fact that higher productivity entailed higher costs and higher borrowings, leading to a positive association with linkages (as explained already). Education (X_4, X_5, X_6, X_7) in the developed villages turned out to be a significant variable with positive sign. This may be explained by the fact that an educated head of the household spends more on education of his children over and above his expenditure on better techniques of production, giving rise to increased demand for informal credit. The per capita debt of households (X_{12}) had the expected positive sign and was statistically significant, implying that an already indebted household had increased probability of linked credit transactions.

Turning to the less developed villages, caste (X_3),

proportion of non-crop income in total income (X_{11}) and ownership of agricultural assets (X_{13}) were the significant variables bearing expected signs, thereby proving important in influencing a household's decision for linked transactions. However, non-agricultural occupations (X_9), although statistically significant, had a positive sign. The income from such occupations as selling milk, working on machines, or as labour/chowkidars is not enough as to reduce borrowing and hence linkage. Same is the case for the variable X_8.

From the results in Table 5 and Table 6 it may be concluded that caste, education, proportion of non-crop income in total income and per capita debt are the important variables which influence a household's decision to go in for linked credit transactions.

CONCLUSIONS

The study has analysed the extent and types of interlinked credit transactions in the informal credit market in Patiala, a district of the Punjab State. The survey revealed that more than 80 percent of the households in the study area obtained credit through linked transactions. Inter-linkage increased with increase in the size of holdings. The situation remained same when the households were divided into two groups: developed villages and less developed village.

Regarding the type of linkage, credit-output linkage was the most dominant in both the developed as well as the less-developed villages. In developed villages, this was followed by credit-labour linkage and in less-developed villages, by credit-output and input linkage. So predominantly, interlinkage involved farmers (particularly large cultivators) and the urban traders and commission agents.

To identify various characteristics influencing a household's decision to opt for linked credit transactions, Maximum likelihood estimates of the Bionomial Probit Model were made. Results for land-owning households and landless class and then for developed and less-developed villages were obtained. It was found that overall, lower education, lower caste, low proportion of income from sources outside agriculture, and higher indebtedness reduce the bargaining power of the borrowers.

These factors have played a very important role in influencing the relation of credit and linkage thereof.

Conclusions, drawn from the experience of the present survey in the specific region (in Punjab) that is agriculturally most advanced, are that the credit institutions are far behind in extending credit to the agricultural sector. These institutions lends on land as a collateral, that too after undergoing a number of formalities and consuming a lot of time of farmers. The implicit costs, when added to the actual rate of interest charged makes institutional credit in many cases costlier than the informal credit. The formal credit agencies have not been able to push the informal lenders out of business, because these lenders have displayed greater foresight in shifting to a better collateral, interlinkage of the agrarian credit market with other agrarian markets–output, input and labour etc., is playing a commendable role in enhancing functioning of the informal credit market in rural India.

Solution for all this is not to weed out the informal credit agencies, replacing by formal ones. Panacea may be integration of these two credit markets. The informal lenders like traders and landlords may be involved in the process of lending by institutions and recovery of such loans. Link of credit with output and input can be worked involving traders. Noting higher interest rates charged by informal credit agencies and lower interest rates by formal agencies with implicit costs (giving rise to interest rates sometimes higher than in the former case) it is suggested that interest rate charged by the formal institutions may be freed. When determined freely in the market, between the formal lender and the borrower, it may work out to be comparable with one in the informal sector. What remains in this context is recovery of such loans. Among financial reforms, steps have been taken towards supervision of banks and recovery of the loans extended as well.

What matters more to the rural poor is the availability and not cost of credit. He is exploited both by the formal as well as informal credit institutions in terms of cost of credit, collateral offered thereof. Visualising the increased lendable funds with banks and their choice for investing in risk-free assets (government securities ahead of SLR requirements), suggests to work out ways for banks to lend to deficit sectors like rural poor by assuring the banks recovery of such loans on one hand and at competitive interest rates on the other hand. This will benefit the agricultural borrower by filling his credit gap and the banks by lending at higher interest rates with low risk and thus increasing their profitability and hence their improved viability.

References

Aleem, 1. (1990); "Imperfect Information, Screening and the Costs of Informal Lending: A study of a Rural Credit Market in Pakistan", *The World Bank Economic Review*, Vol. 4, pp. 329-349.

Bandhopadhyay, A. (1984): *An Analysis of Agricultural Credit in West Bengal*, Agricole Co., New Delhi.

Bardhan, P.K. (1984): *Land, Labour and Rural Poverty: Essays in Development Economics*, Oxford University Press, Delhi.

Bardhan, P.K. (1989), "A Note on Interlinked Rural Economic Arrangements", in P.K. Bardhan (ed.,) *The Economic Theory of Agrarian Institutions*, Oxford Claredon Press, pp. 237-242.

Bardhan, P.K. and Rudra, A. (1978): "Interlinkage of Land, Labour and Credit Relations: A analysis of Village Survey Data in East India", *Economic and Political Weekly*, Vol. 13, Annual Number, February.

Basu, K. (1989): "Rural Credit Markets: The Structure of Interest Rates, Exploitation and Efficiency", in Bardhan, P.K. (ed.), *The Economic Theory of Agrarian Institutions*, Oxford Claredeon Press, New York.

Bell, C. (1990): "Interactions between Institutional and Informal Credit Agencies in Rural India", *The World Bank Economic Review*, Vol. 4, No. 3, September, pp. 297-327.

Bell, C. and Srinivasan, T.N. (1989): "Interlinked Transactions in Rural Markets: An Empirical Study of Andhra Pradesh, Bihar and Punjab", *Oxford Bulletin of Economics and Statistics*, Vol. 51, No. 1, pp. 73-83.

Collier, P. and Lal, D. (1985). *Labour and Poverty in Kenya 1900-1980*, Oxford University Press, London.

Darling, M. (1925): *The Punjab Peasant in Prosperity and Debt*, Oxford University Press, London.

Floro, S.L. and Yotopoulos, P.A. (1991): *Informal Credit Markets and the New Institutional Economics: The Case of Phillipine Agriculture*, Westview Press Inc., Boulder.

Gangapadhyay, S. and Sengupta, K. (1987), "Usury and Collateral Pricing: Towards an Alternative Explanation", *Cambridge Journal of Economics*, Vol. 11, No. 1, pp. 47-56.

Ghate, P.B. (1992): "Interaction between the Formal and Informal Financial Sectors: The Asian Experience", *World Development*, Vol. 20, No. 6, pp. 859-872.

Jones, W.O. (1980); "Agricultural Trade within Tropical Africa: Achievements and Difficulties", in Bates, R.H. and Lofchia, M.F. (eds.), *Agricultural Development in Africa: Issues of Public Policy*, Praeger, New York.

Kutty, H. (1988); "Coconut Marketing in Kerala," *M.Phil Dissertation*, Centre for Development Studies, Trivendrum.

Sarap, K. (1987): "Small Farmers' Transactions in Rural Credit Markets in Western Orissa", *Journal of Peasant Studies*, Vol. 15, No. 1, pp. 83-107.

Sarap, K. (1990): "Factors Affecting Small Farmers' Access to Institutional Credit in Rural Orissa, India", *Development and Change*, Vol. 21, No. 2, pp. 281-307.

Siamwalla, A., *et al.*, (1990): "The Thai Rural Credit System: Public Subsidies, Private Information and Segmented Markets", *The World Bank Economic Review*, Vol 4., No. 3, pp. 271-298.

Swaminathan, M. (1991): "Segmentation, Collateral Undervaluation, and the Rate of Interest in Agrarian Credit Markets: Some Evidence from Two Villages in South India", *Cambridge Journal of Economics*, Vol. 15, pp. 161-178.

Wharton, C. (1962): "Marketing Merchandising and Moneylending: A Note on Middleman Monospsony in Malaya", *Malayan Economic Review*, Vol. 7, October.

PART D

INDIAN MONEY MARKET UNDER ECONOMIC REFORMS

9

Emerging Money-Market in India under Economic Reforms: The Need for Integration with Foreign Exchange Market

V.N. Attri and Neera Verma

Innovative variations in money supply do have their impact in the economy. The evidences show that the rise in money supply has a positive effect on output and price level though it does not have a direct effect on employment level. Sustainable economic growth with low level of inflation is possible, if the Monetary Policy acts as an independent policy instrument. In that situation the Central Bank of the country can decide about its priorities in a better and effective way. During 1980s, the domestic price stability became the major objective, to be achieved by the Central Banks in almost all the countries.

In achieving the objective of domestic price stability; the exchange rate stability is also needed on two accounts; (i) the volatility in exchange rate gives spurt to inflationary expectations; (ii) it adds to the monetary expansion in an economy, if the exchange rate is arbitrarily fixed by the Central Bank of a country. Therefore, the synthesis of domestic price stability alongwith exchange rate stability is needed to have a sustainable economic growth.

The basic objective of the paper is to examine the developments in Indian Money Market over the period under study in the light of above discussion. The paper has been divided into four sections. Section I deals with interconnections between Money Market and Exchange Market and the reforms in the Money Market in India. Section II has been devoted to India's experience with Money Market in pre-and post-liberalization period. The empirical content has been added to the paper by applying simple and multiple regression models in section III. Section IV discusses the main conclusions of the study.

I

Several empirical studies have applied endogenous growth theory to show the possibility of a close association between the level of development in the financial sector and growth. Generally, it is assumed that financial development helps to improve the efficiency of capital allocation. This happens due to the possibility of choosing more productive investments through improved management of liquidity risks (*Bencivenga and Smith, 1991*), by diversifying more investor's protfolios efficiency (Levine 1991). J.C. Berthelemy and A. Varoudakis (1996) in their paper have shown that the financial underdevelopment may act as a severe obstacle to growth in such developing countries where financial repression exists. In such countries, economic openness does not seem to exert a positive impact on growth, while government expenditure has a positive effect. Therefore, it seems desirable to establish as early as possible policies that would avoid a heavy repression of the financial system to be able to pursue optimal policies in other areas.

The financial system is a broad term including Money Market, Capital Market and also the foreign exchange Market. Traditionally, the external and internal equilibrium in the economy can be achieved in a unique position when Money Market (LM), Real Market (IS) and the Foreign Exchange Market (FE) are in equilibrium. This is really a difficult proposition as according to Macro-disequilibrium Economics, we know that the disequilibrium in the different markets exist due to prevailing distortions. Under such circumstances, the main task of the policy-makers becomes removal of these restrictions by adopting right policies so as to put the economy on the right path that leads to equilibrium in the different markets.

The exchange rate policy has a very important role to play in keeping the inflation level low. Empirical studies indicate that the successful stabilization programmes in most cases, began with a pegged exchange rate and then moving gradually towards flexibility in the exchange rate regime over time. Sebastian Edwards (1993) have shown that in countries with a reputation for stability, the adoption of a fixed exchange rate has introduced financial discipline. However, as this reputation which we have measured by past inflation, becomes weaker, the constraining effects of the fixed exchange rate begin to rapidly disappear.

After the collapse of Bretton Wood System (1973), the industrial countries adopted the freely Floating Exchange Rate System which was further followed by the developing countries in 1980s and 1990s as consequence of liberalization of their economies. According to December, 1990 issue of the IMF's International Financial Statistics, the proportion of LDC members of the fund that had some type of fixed exchange rate had declined to 67 per cent which further fell to 57 per cent in 1993. The existing literature shows that the stabilization of inflation can be achieved through pegged exchange rate as well as floating exchange rate. The exchange rate policy should ensure the long term international competitiveness of the economy by controlling the growing overvaluation of the currency.

Exchange rate management should meet the needs of the exporters by having a favourable exchange rate; but at the same time it must prevent monetary expansion in order to maintain price stability. Hence, there should be an integration between the Money Market and Foreign Exchange Market.

The financial sector in India has been repressive like any other developing country. The repressiveness of the financial sector is characterized by: (i) interest rate ceiling and negative real interest rates; (ii) pervasive credit rationing, (iii) selective central bank rediscounting of commercial sectors for favoured sector; (iv) Lack of credit-rating services and restricted entry in the financial sector; and (v) Rapid growth of high powered money and inflation.

During pre-liberalized era the Money Market was highly regulatory and controlled. Monetary policy and monetary expansion have been largely determined by the government's borrowing requirements as such the distinction between objectives and instruments has been blurred. Historically, SLR and CRR have been the main instruments of monetary policy. Rising fiscal deficits over the 1980s made the monetised deficit a major factor driving growth of money Supply. The long term average of Broad Money (M_3) has been 17.2 per cent since 1980-81 whereas it was contained to 15.9 per cent in 1996-97 due to the reforms introduced in the Money Market in India since 1991. The process of reforms in the financial sector was initiated in 1980s especially with the appointment of Chakravarti Committee (1985).

Since the mid-eighties, Monetary reforms continued the processs of modernising the instruments of monetary control to make them more conducive for the application of monetary policy in a market economy. Though administered interest rates continued to play a role, they were made more flexible. The restrictions on bank advances have been liberalized to enhance the flexibility of Bank operations. The guidelines for the opening of private banks as well as foreign banks were liberalized.

In order to raise the liquidity of funds for investment, the interest rates were reduced; Capital Adequacy norms were introduced. The SLR and CRR have been reduced. A reduction of the CRR also reduces the implicit taxation on banks and increases their potential profitability. There has been further liberalization of rules governing consortium finance in the case of multiple bank lending. The rules related with selective credit controls; priority sector advances, and foreign exchange transactions were liberalised to ensure the flexibility and competitiveness. The reforms in the foreign exchange market includes: the unification of exchange rates; convertibility on current account and selective convertibility on capital account.

As a consequence of financial liberalization and autonomy of financial sector, the credit risk, interest rate risk and foreign exchange risk have increased and will become even more critical. Hence the risk management techniques should be evolved; and future course of reforms should be in the field of Risk Management. These precautions should be taken into account for the efficient evoking of the Market Mechanism.

II

Indian Money Market prior to liberalization has been regulatory and controlled leading to financial repression. The financial repression hypothesis as developed by McKinnon (1973) Shaw (1973) and Fry (1982, 1988) says that inefficiency in financial systems arises due to the failure of government policy. It is believed that financial liberalization leads to financial deepening, improved efficiency and results in lower spreads between borrowing and lending rates etc. Therefore introducing the financial reforms in a developing economy like India would ensure higher rate of economic growth.

The objective of the Money Market is to provide adequate and timely funds at reasonable rates for industry, trade and commerce. It also acts as a medium for the effective execution of the monetary policy to be implemented by the Central Bank of the country. India does not have an independent central bank and the responsibility for major decisions on monetary policy rests with the Finance Ministry. In 1960s, the market interest rates and the allocation of funds (Credit) to the different sectors of the economy were determined arbitrarily by the RBI in consultation with government. The independence of RBI was severely eroded after bank nationalisation. The range of monetary policy instruments in India has been wide covering both direct (quantity) and indirect (price) approaches.

The developments in Money Market during pre-liberalization (i.e. 1950-51 to 1980-81) which period can be better understood and analysed with the help of Table 1.

Table 1 reveals that during this period, with the growth of M_1 and M_3, the wholesale price index has also increased. The financial development has also taken place in India as M_2/GDP ratio has increased from 25.9 per cent to 27.9 per cent in 1975.

During the whole period i.e. (1960-80) the real interest rates has either been very low or negative as indicated by Table 2.

TABLE 1

Monetary Indicators, Period, Averages: 1960-61 to 1974-75

Period	M_1g	M_3g	WPI_g	V_{11}	V_3
1960-61 to 1964-65	7.5	7.7	5.3	6.39	4.22
1965-66 to 1969-70	8.3	10.9	7.2	7.42	4.51
1970-71 to 1974-75	12.6	15.5	13.3	7.21	3.90

M_1g : Average annual percentage growth of narrow money.
M_3g : Average annual percentage growth of Broad Money.
WPI_g : Average annual wholesale price Inflation.
V_{11}: Velocity of M_{11}.
V_3 : Velocity of M_3.
Adopted from Vijay Joshi & I.M.D. Little, "*India: Macroeconomics and Political Economy—1964-1991*", (1994).

These low or negative real interest rates have a bearing on the economic growth. Generally, it is hypothesized that higher rate of growth is associated with high positive real interest rates. Though, this relationship is not direct and simple, even then, several empirical studies have proved that the determination of interest rates by market forces and ensuring positive real interest rates is required in the developing economies where financial system is generally repressive.

In an attempt to make Indian Money Market efficient through market mechanisms, Indian government appointed Chakravarty Committee. The Committee suggested a move towards a system in which the government would meet its financing needs from the market at market-related interest rates rather than from the Reserve Bank of India. By and large, the Money Market in India has been distorted and excessively controlled as the government intervened too often in the working of the RBI till 1980s. The oil shocks (1973, 1979) and other external factors compelled the government to pursue tight monetary policy which has adversely affected long term growth. However, the inflationary pressure was successfully kept under control. To what extent, low inflation during this period has led to low growth rates and financial repression needs further investigation. But the liberalization of the financial system including Money

TABLE 2

Behaviour of Money Market Rate and Real Interest Rates in India : 1960-1991

Year	*Money Market Rate*	*Real Interest Rate*	*Year*	*Money Market Rate*	*Real Interest Rate*
1960	3.67	2.04	1976	11.28	20.65
1961	4.35	2.70	1977	10.18	1.64
1962	3.70	0.48	1978	8.05	5.41
1963	3.76	0.64	1979	8.47	1.94
1964	4.00	-8.28	1980	7.24	-3.73
1965	6.28	-2.67	1981	8.61	-3.88
1966	4.37	-5.80	1982	7.27	-0.58
1967	5.36	-7.25	1983	8.30	-3.21
1968	3.90	-0.97	1984	9.95	1.52
1969	3.92	2.18	1985	10.00	4.16
1970	5.68	0.55	1986	9.97	1.16
1971	6.30	3.00	1987	8.83	0.94
1972	4.69	-0.48	1988	15.00	5.11
1973	6.64	-9.47	1989	12.57	6.09
1974	13.52	-11.10	1990	15.57	6.12
1975	10.00	4.16	1991	19.35	4.78

Adopted from, V.N. Attri and Neera Verma, "Development of Financial System and Economic Growth in India: 1960-61". *Indian Economic Association, Conference Vol. 1994*, pp. 11-16.

Market and Capital Market will certainly enhance the prospects of higher growth rates as a consequence of increased financial efficiency. For the last three years the growth rate of GDP has been varying between 6-7 per ecnt. This will also result into the independence of the RBI, so crucial for the higher growth of output, low inflation and limited volatility in exchange rate.

In the post-liberalization period, efforts have been made to soften the allocative regulations, by moving towards market determined interest rates, hardening of the prudential regulations and providing better access to money and capital markets by framing oriented rules and regulation. In order to make these markets internationally competitive so as to attract high foreign capital flows. It is in this context that the integration of foreign exchange market and money market is needed. This trend was absent during 1960s, 1970 and also in early 1980s in India (Rangarajan, C. 1982, 1988; 1990; and 1994); and Narasimham Committee (1991), contributed a lot in establishing the foundation of financial liberalisation in India. The Narasimham Committee recommended that banking sector, capital markets and financial institutions should be made competitive, efficient and profitable. Flexibility in the financial system should be introduced and it must be free from existing 'distortions' in order to achieve equilibrium in all the financial markets. I.G. Patel (1993) and D.N. Ghosh (1993) further made significant contributions to the process of financial reforms in the country.

As discussed in brief in section I of the present paper, the exchange rate policy in India has been developed to be used as an inflation-anchor. Whether fixed exchange rate or fully floating exchange rate is an appropriate choice? This question has different answers. In some countries during reforms flexible exchange rate has been successful in curbing the inflation while in others credit goes to the fixed exchange rate. In India, the picture becomes clear with the help of the Table 3.

It is clear from the Table 3 that the impact of exchange-rate on inflation has been very low; it has been primarily linked with money supply growth, fiscal-deficits and food-production. Even then, the rate of inflation under floating exchange-rate has been low as compared to fixed exchange-rate.

But if we view the movements in real effective exchange rate (REER), certainly, the policy has been a failure during 1960s—leading to the devaluation of June, 1966. Again, in 1970s and 1980s the move towards nominal fixed exchange rate eroded the competitiveness of our exports, current account deficit persisted, and foreign debt grew rapidly. Not only this the total foreign exchange reserves also come down to the minimum critical level—leading to the crisis of 1991.

After the adoption of flexible exchange rate policy in 1992, the foreign exchange reserves started growing. In 1990-91, the

TABLE 3

Inflation in different Exchange Rate Regimes: 1960-61 to 1996-97*

Regime	*Years*	*Average inflation (per cent)*
Pegged exchange-rate		
(i) Adjustable Peg	1960-61 to 1982-83	7.9
(ii) Crawling Peg	1983-84 to 1990-91	7.5
Comparison (ii) Adjustable Peg	1960-61 to 1971-72 and 1976-77 to 1982-83	6.8
Crawling Peg More Flexible	1972-73 to 1975-76 and 1983-84 to 1990-91	9.5
Other managed Floating	1992-93 to 1996-97	7.3

* Adopted from Vijay Joshi. IMD Little "India: Macro Economics and Political Economy; 1964-1991" (1994) with some modifications of our own study on "Exchange-Rate Policy Inflation and Economic Growth in Developing Countries", unpublished.

total reserves were Rs. 11416.4 crores and in 1995-96 they rose to Rs. 74384.6 crores seven times higher than the year 1990-91. The unification of the exchange rate and the introduction of convertibility on current account (in full) and capital account on selective basis are some of the welcome measures related with foreign exchange market under post-liberalization period. Very recently, Tarapore Committee recommended convertibility on capital account.

After having a brief discussion[2] on the developments in money market and foreign exchange market during the period under study, we now turn to the econometric analysis in section III.

III

The monetary authorities and the central banks generally believe that the foreign exchange markets can't process the information efficiently and hence there arises a need for their intervention. In order to see the impact of foreign exchange markets on the inflationary process in India, we have used "foreign exchange reserve" as a proxy to exchange rate regimes. It is generally viewed by the economists that the flexible exchange rate policy raises the volume of foreign exchange reserve if followed by liberalized financial market(s). We have taken the absolute time series data for broad money (M_3) foreign exchange reserves and whole sale price index (1985=100) from the various issues of IMF's International Financial Statistics and Economic Surveys, published by Ministry of Finance, Government of India, New Delhi.

TABLE 4

Regression Results showing the impact of Money Supply (M_3); and Foreign Exchange Reserves of Inflation (WP_1)

Dependent Variable	*Period*	*Constant term*	*'b'*	*R^2*	*Adj.*	*F-statistics*
WPI (QMS_3)	1960-92	29.889 (11.03)	0.049 (20.76)	0.932	0.930	431.00
	1950-70	12.177 (5.66)	0.144 (4.17)	0.65	0.62	17.45
	1970-80	26.782 (7.91)	0.072 (6.96)	0.84	0.82	48.54
	1980-90	59.453 (17.50)	0.033 (14.27)	0.957	0.953	283.86
	1980-92	59.16 (41.12)	0.055 (43.89)	0.99	0.99	1926.39
WPI-f (Forex)	1960-92	31.067 (3.257)	0.013 (4.688)	0.41	0.39	21.98
	1960-70	15.175 (2.85)	0.011 (0.97)	0.09	-0.00	0.94
	1970-80	35.910 (9.380)	0.041 (3.981)	0.63	0.59	15.85
	1980-90	142.409 (7.263)	-0.009 (-2.090)	0.32	0.25	4.37
	1980-92	49.97 (5.615)	-0.006 (-0.908)	0.06	-0.01	0.827

Figures in parentheses are t-statistics.

TABLE 5

Multiple Regression Results showing the impact of Money Supply (M_3) and Foreign Exchange Reserves on Inflation (WPI)

Model Specification	*Period*	*Constant term*	*b_1 Coefficient*	*b_2 Coefficient*	*R^2*	*Adj. R^2*	*F-statistics*
WPI=f	1960-92	22.537	0.044	0.004	0.967	0.964	447.48
(QMS_3, FOREX)		(9.740)	(22.609)	(5.662)			
AR (I)	1960-70	6.872	0.278	-0.006	0.95	0.94	80.94
		(5.319)	(9.262)	(-1.603)			
	1970-80	17.02	0.161	0.003	0.92	0.90	50.62
		(4.431)	(5.591)	(-2.558)			
	1980-92	59.620	0.033	0.033	0.99	0.98	464.15
		(14.67)	(24.94)	(-0.04)			
Lagged	1960-92	23.415	0.051	0.004	0.969	0.967	465.54
Results		(10.378)	(23.846)	(5.950)			

Figures in parentheses are t-statistics.

Simple and multiple regressions have been run by removing the serial correlation in the data. The results are presented in Tables 4 and 5.

Table 4 shows that money supply (M_3) has been crucial in raising the inflationary pressure in India during the period under study; the sub-period (1960-70) has much higher 'b' coefficient as compared to all other sub-periods. Also over the subsequent decades, the Reserve Bank of India became conscious of the inflation problem and the price stability at domestic level became the main objective of the monetary authority.

The foreign exchange reserves have not been a significant determining factor of inflation in India over the period under study as revealed by Table 5; the result of ignoring the foreign exchange market by the monetary authorities is reflected in the rate of economic growth during the period under study. It is also indicative of the type of policies, i.e. achieving industrialization through import-substitution till the mid of 1980s; therefore, the model developed by Vijay Joshi (1994) explains the inflationary process in a better way.

In this model, the import prices happen to be significant

variable. We feel that integrating the foreign exchange market with monetary policies would have been more growth-oriented. The very low and negative values of b_2 coefficient in Table 5 reveal the fact that fixed exchange rate regime in India has been successful to contain the inflationary pressure. This is in accordance with the latest theoretical developments which view the fixed exchange-rate policy better in a country with low inflation record in the past as in case of India, when compared to other developing countries.

But when we run foreign exchange reserves as an instrument variable for the period 1980-92, the regression equation shows:

	R^2	R^2
49.97 + 0.003 FOREX + 1.160 AR (1)	0.992	0.990
(5.61) (0.0456) (30.73)	F-Starts	
	(582.82)	

The above equation implies that the foreign exchange reserve as an instrument variable does influence the inflation, though the values are not statistically significant. The relationship, in absence of liberaized money market and foreign exchange market, between inflation and foreign exchange reserves appears to be weak and uncertain. The relationship is indirect and unclear which needs further investigation of quarterly data.

IV

The main conclusions of the study are as follows:

(i) The study reveals that there is no clear and definite relationship between exchange rate regime(s) and inflation. Generally, in the initial period of liberalization the fixed exchange rate is preferable to flexible exchange rate regime. Gradually, it must be replaced by flexible exchange rate regime as it has other positive effects on the economy such as high growth rates in addition to curbing the inflation. The use of exchange rate regimes vary from country to country. There can be no general rule.

(ii) Money supply has been a powerful variable in India

during the period under study. But the sub-period wise results show that its impact has been declining due to better management of the money supply (M_3) by the RBI and the financial liberalization. The liberalization of money market such as deregulation of interest rates is having a positive impact on the economy.

(iii) One of the indirect policy implication of the study is to increase the independence of the RBI, so that in absence of political intervention the Bank can follow a judicious and right monetary policy including the better management of the foreign exchange market. The recent behaviour of the foreign exchange market confirms the fact that the integration of the two markets is a must to ensure high growth rate in the economy with low-inflation level.

The future agenda for research requires a deep analysis in this area by analysing quarterly time series data on foreign-exchange markets so as to ascertain the efficiency of foreign exchange market via-a-vis money market under liberalized regime.

Notes and References

1. The details of the reforms in money market, foreign exchange market and other components of financial sector can be found in the various issues of Economic Survey published by Ministry of Finance, Govt. of India, New Delhi.
2. For details of the reform of the money market, capital markets and foreign-exchange markets, see various issues of Economic Surveys, published by Govt. of India, Ministry of Finance, New Delhi.

References

Attri, V.N. and Neera Verma (1994): "Development of Financial System and Economic Growth in India, 1960-61" *Indian Economic Journal,* Conference Vol.

Bencivenga, V.R. & Smith, B.D. (1991): "Financial International and Endogenous Growth", *Review of Economic Studies,* 58, 195-209.

Bergosen, C. Fred & Williamson John (1983): "Exchange Rates and Trade Policy", William Cline (ed.) Trade Policy in the 1980s, Washington D.C. Institute for International Economic, pp. 99-120.

Dombysch, Rudigee (1986): "Flexible Exchange Rates and Excess Capital Mobility", *Brookings Papers on Economic Activity,* pp. 209-219.

Edwards, Sebastian (1996): "Exchange Rates and the Political Economy of Macroeconomic Discipline", *American Economic Review* May 1996, 86 (2), pp. 159-163.

Frankel J. and Rose, Andrew (1995): "Empirical Research on Nominal Exchange Rates". Gene Grossman and Kenneth Rogoff (eds.) *Handbook of International Economics*, Amsterdam: North Holland, pp. 1989-1729.

Friedman, Milton (1953): "The Case for Flexible Exchange Rate. Milton Friedman (ed.), *Essays in Positive Economies*, Chicago, University of Chicago Press, 1953, pp. 157-203.

I.C. Berthelemy & A. Varoudakis (1996): "Economic Growth Convergence Clubs, and the Role of Financial Development", *Oxford Economic Papers*, 48, 300-328.

Levine, R. (1991): "Stock Markets Growth and Tax-Policy", *Journal of Finance*, 46, 1445-65.

McKinnon, Ronald (1998): Monetary and Exchange Rate Policies for International Financial Stability", *Journal of Economic Perspectives*, Winter 1988, 2(1) pp. 83-103.

Michael Mehin & Kok-Hui Tan (1996): "Foreign Exchange Market Bid-ask Spreads and the Market Price of Social Unrest", *Oxford Economic Papers* (48), (1990)· 329-41.

Mussa, Michael (1990): "Exchange Rates in theory and in Reality". *International Finance*. No. 179, Princeton, NJ: International Finance Sector, Princeton University.

Tobin, James (1978): "A Proposal for International Monetary Reform", *Eastern Economic Journal*, July/October 4(3-4) pp. 153-159.

Williamson, John (1987): "Exchange Rate Management: The Role of Target Zones". *American Economic Review*, May.

10

Money Market Instruments: The Case of Certificate of Deposit

Vijay Laxmi Chari

The growth and development of the financial sector usually takes place in tandem with the overall growth and development of an economy. The importance, activities and functions of the financial sector acquire an added dimension as the international economic linkages of the economy expand and diversify. The development of money market becomes crucial at this point for two main reasons. The changes due to reforms in the money market would be affected by and effect the financial sector initially and the whole economy thereafter. India has experienced a lot of regulatory changes and freedom from control of monetary authority in the money market during the recent years. This has followed the removal of restriction from all spheres of economic activities. The changes in the money market depend, to a large extent, on the performance of the money market instruments. Several instruments were revived and some new introductions were made in the Indian money market since 1990. One such instrument was the Certificate of Deposit (hereafter referred to as CD).

The main aim of this paper is to delineate the special

characteristics of certificate of deposit, keeping in view the specificity of the money market, explore its position in the major money markets of the world, trace its ues in the Indian money market and discuss its future role.

THE MONEY MARKET

Basically all financial markets facilitate the transfer of real economic resources from the lender to the borrower. (Henning, 1975) The characteristics which distinguish money markets from other financial markets are :

(1) It is a short term market with transaction periods ranging from three days to one year.

(2) The volume of transactions is usually large. The minimum size of each transaction being fixed by the monetary regularity authority and is in denominationss of lakhs of units of a currency.

(3) Due to the large volume and short duration of transactions, the number of players are limited. Regulatory impositions also restrict the entry of players besides limiting the freedom of the permitted players.

The money market thus addresses the large volume, short term funds requirements of borrowers, so that they need to hold less money for their temporary unexpected cash drain. It provides an excellent opportunity to the players to park their surplus funds temporarily with at least an assured minimal return. It helps in reducing brokerage fees, search costs and other transaction costs incurred in buying and selling short term debt instruments. It also enables finance of long term needs through roll-overs.

Owing to special characteristics of the money market, new instruments evolved to facilitate the trading in the money market. They usually bear a different rate of interest and maturity duration compared to other financial market instruments. But over the above all this, they are distinguished by their highly liquid character. Thus they are a closer substitute to money than other financial assets (Auerbach, 1989).

The traditional money market in the organized sector was confirmed to the inter-bank call money market. Business organizations soon found themselves in need of large short term funds or often wanted to avail of an opportunity to profitably park their surplus funds for short duration. Thus there existed a demand as well as supply source for money market funds. The routing of operations through banks was found to be inadequate. This led to a natural evolution of several other money market instruments in which the main players were business organizations with banks usually adopting the role of an intermediary. The most common instruments were:

- Government Treasury Bills,
- Commercial Paper,
- Intercorporate deposits,
- Bankers' acceptance,
- Repos and
- Certificates of deposit.

The capital market instruments (long term securities) are also sometimes traded in the money market at the fag end of their lives.

THE CERTIFICATE OF DEPOSIT

It is a negotiable promissory note which is issued by a banking company in the name of the purchaser (usually a business corporation). It is a fixed term instrument bearing a fixed rate of interest. The interest rate offered is either determined by the regulatory authority or based on the overall money market rates. It is issued in large denominations, the minimum deposit having a floor limit prescribed by the monetary authority. The banks redeem the deposit at full maturity only. They also do not accept it as a collateral for any further borrowings. The CDs are generally traded in the secondary market, on yield to maturity basis. They do not affect the borrowing limits of a corporation with the issuing bank. Compared to other money market instruments, the CDs have the following advantage:

(1) They generally offer a higher rate of interest than treasury bills.
(2) They are a safe parking place for surplus funds, compared to most of the other money market instruments with the exception of Treasury bills.
(3) They can be sold off in the secondary market in case urgent funds are required. In this case neither the seller nor the purchaser loose on interest as they are transacted on yield to maturity basis.

This instrument was introduced in 1966 and its use became popular from the decade of seventies.

CDs in the London Money Market

The banks are the primary source of CDs. These are issued in multiples of ten thousand pounds with deposits going up to a million pounds. The maturity period ranges from three months to five years. Now they are issued for an even shorter period of 28 days. The accounting year is of 365 days. Payment of interest is without deduction of tax. The CD market is an unsecured market without there being a lender of the last resort. It is actively traded in the secondary market on yield to maturity basis. The Discount houses are active players in the secondary market for CDs.

CDs are also issued in other currencies such as dollar CDs. The minimum denominations for different currencies are different currencies are different. The secondary market in such CDs is confined to those issued by London banks and CDs issued by foreign banks can not be traded in the secondary market. CDs can not be denominated in any currency except the pound without the prior sanction of the monetary regulatory authority. The interest on these CDs is calculated on the basis of a 360 day year. The secondary market dealers in such CDs can only be London based and they require a clearance from The Bank of England to operate in it. (Maycock, 1983).

The US CD Market

These are more popular in the US than in England as they are the most utilized Money market instrument after Treasury Bills. The maturity period ranges from seven days to 18 months.

The issue sources are four types of financial intermediaries. US banks issuing domestic CDs denominated in dollars; Euro-dollar CDs issued by banks outside US; Yankee CDs issued by US branches of foreign banks and thrift CDs issued by domestic thrifts. A special provision in the US is that Variable Rate CDs can be issued with generally longer duration of 12 to 18 months. For these the maturity period is subdivided into several parts. The interest rate for each sub-period is fixed as a spread over some other basic rate such as the inter-bank call rate. They are also exempt from reserve requirement. The CDs generally carry a higher rate of interest than the T bills but have a higher risk of default than them (Auerbach, 1989).

Interestingly CDs are not traded in the German, French or Swiss money markets. They are traded in the Japanese money market where they came into use in 1979. They provide an avenue for arbitrage between inter bank market and the open market. They are mainly issued by the city banks and purchased by corporations and local corporations. Non-residents are also permitted to trade in them. They are also traded in the Gensaki market. (*Dufey & Krishnan; Aftain and Bompaire; Corti, Allen,* 1983).

CDs in the Indian Money Market

The Indian money market was confined to the inter-bank call money market in the organized sector for a long time. The informal money market did exist but was outside the organized sector and usually catered to specific local requirements. The change in the Indian money market was initiated by the recommendations of the Chakravarty Committee while reviewing the working of the Monetary System. On the basis of these recommendations a committee was set up by the Reserve Bank of India in September 1986, under the chairmanship of Sri N. Vaghul for a comprehensive review of the Indian money market. This Committee recommended that the following major changes in the Indian money market should take place keeping in view the following objectives:

(1) It should provide an equilibrating mechanism for evening out short term surpluses and deficits.

(2) It should provide a focal point for central bank intervention for influencing liquidity in the economy.

(3) It should provide reasonable access to the users of short term money to meet their requirements at a realistic price.

These reforms were envisaged because "in the context of other vital changes in the economy, a significant element of rationalization of the monetary and banking system would be inevitable" (Vaghul, 1986, p. 11).

The Committee, however, did not recommend the introduction of CDs then as the short term deposit rates needed to be aligned with other rates in the system first. The absence of an active secondary market were also considered as a limitation. The full recommendations of the Vaghul Committee on Certificates of Deposit are reproduced in Appendix A.

In view of these recommendations, RBI formulated a scheme in June 1989 for the issue of CDs by scheduled commercial banks (excluding RRBs). The banks were allowed to issue CDs at a freely determined discount rate from the face value. Thus the interest rate on CDs were delinked from the administered interest rate.

During the decade of nineties several changes have taken place in the regulations for CDs. At present the minimum size of CDs has been reduced to Rs. 10 lakhs in multiples of five lakhs (*RBI*, 1997). Thus even small amounts of surplus cash with the corporations can be parked here. They can be issued to individuals, corporations, companies, trust funds, associations etc. They can also be issued to NRIs but on a non-repatriable basis. Yet they still attract a stamp duty which is needed for each transaction of a CD. They can be traded in the secondary market only after 45 days of initial issue. The banks are still required to maintain the usual reserve on the CDs, although the limit on outstanding CDs has been scrapped for the banks. Apart from scheduled commercial banks, six financial institutions, namely SIDBI, IDBI, IFCI, ICICI, IRBI and EXIM bank have been permitted since 1993 to issue CDs. The banks still can not grant loans against CDs. They are redeemed by the banks after full maturity period. This instrument still retains the character of informality as it is issued on inter party negotiation basis for lack of a unique selection method for acceptance of bids. The banks fix a floor level of interest/discount for CDs. These can be negotiated only in exceptional circumstances. In India, every bank branch has to refer to its office at Mumbai (the main money market centre) for a change in the rates offered for CDs. The main player in the secondary market for CDs is the Discount and Finance House of India (a subsidiary of Reserve Bank of India) DFHI operates as the market maker in the CD market. It quotes both bid and offer rates for CDs. It settles the transactions on spot basis. (*Khan,* 1996).

The CDs have seen a lot of ups and downs during their short period of use in the Indian money market since 1990. One important aspect which has not changed is that the banks fix the interest/discount rate on CDs on the basis of call money rates in the inter-bank market. The following Table 1 shows the relation between the various rates in the money market.

TABLE 1

Relative Rates of Return in Major Financial Markets

Item	*Last Week/Fortnight of Month (Percent per annum)*		
	Mar. 1995	*Mar. 1996*	*Jan. 1997*
1. Call money rate (Mumbai) (DFHI Average Lending Rate)	16.10	16.28	3.21
2. 91-day Treasury Bills (auction) (Cut-off yield)	11.90	12.97	7.50
3. 364-day Treasury Bills (Cut-off yield)	11.94	12.97	10.10
4. Certificates of Deposit (middle rate)	12.50	17.13	
5. Commercial Paper (Middle discount rate)	14.50	20.15	11.69

Source: RBI Bulletin, February 1997.

The table shows that the rates on most of the money market instruments increased with an increase in the call money rate. With the downward trend in the call money rates, the rate offered on CDs has also shown a decline. In general the discount rate is in the range of 13% when the DFHI call money rate is around 10.9% (IBA, Jan. 1997). In fact the banks now offer a higher rate of interest on term deposits. The term deposits can also be used as a collateral. But they can not be negotiated in the secondary market. Moreover, they do not attract stamp duty and therefore, are less costly for the banks. The effective marginal cost of term deposits for banks works out to be in the range of 11.508 to 16.270 with interest ranging from 10% to 13% Compared to that the cost for CDs comes out to be 18.651 calculated at an interest rate of 14% per annum (Jain, 1996, p. 160). Even if the CDs do provide a hedge against the call money risk, they are still comparatively costlier than other deposits for Indian banks Considering the bulk denominations of CDs they prove to be highly unprofitable for the banks. Naturally the banks are not actively soliciting CDs but encourage term and other types of deposits which provide higher yield and are less costly.

During 1993-94 when there was an excess shortage of liquidity in the money market, both the banks and the corporations were facing a cash crunch, the interest rate on CDs went sky high. It was during this period that CDs became very popular. It was, however, found that most of the CD holders retained them up to maturity and consequently there was hardly any secondary market trading in them. The banks also discovered that when CDs were encouraged by them as a hedge against the call money market risk, the profit which would have accrued due to their secondary market trading did not materialise. Even during the short maturity period of CDs the call money rates were too volatile for CDs to provide adequate hedge. The purchasers also were slightly discouraged by the fact that these could not be used as collateral for further bank loan. Over and above all this the reserve requirement and the stamp duty both cut into the profit earning capacity of the banks through this route. (Handa, 1995) Thus the popularity of CDs slowly declined and in its place other instruments such as commercial paper became more popular. With the decline of rates in the call money market the rates offered by banks on CDs have also shown a down trend so much so that the rates on Commercial Paper are now higher than those on the CDs. The following Table 2 shows the latest trends in the money market rates in India.

TABLE 2

Money Market Rates in India

Item	*Rates (% per annum)*	*Volume (this week in Rs. Crores)* *16-6-97*
Call money	4.25 - 10.50	6345.00
Repos	5.00 - 9.65	217.00
91 days T Bill	5.10 - 7.13	68.47
364 days T Bill	5.48 - 9.39	239.05
CP	8.35 - 9.80	25.00
CD	6.80 - 8.00	30.00
		June 2, 1997
Call Money	4.25 - 8.25	8341.00
Repos	5.00 - 9.25	82.50
91 days T bill	3.99 - 6.73	57.50
364 days T bill	5.24 - 9.52	70.60
CD	12.0	N.A.
CP	11.50	N.A.

Economic Times, 16.6.1997 and 2.6.1997.

FUTURE PROSPECTS

The examples of trading in CDs quoted above from the major financial markets of the world show that this instrument is popular in US but not in London. Both are well developed financial markets. Besides there are some well developed markets like that of Germany where this is not in use at all. The Indian money market is still at a nascent stage compared to these markets. The question is what should be the future of this instrument? The options available are :

(1) To let the market deal with it on its own without any further interference from RBI.

(2) To abolish the CD all together as it has not shown

a very consistent performance and let other instruments such as the Commercial Paper be encouraged in its place.

(3) To avoid the above two extreme steps, another alternative could be to alter the method of trading in CDs to make them more popular.

State intervention may be frowned upon now in any sector of the economy with the changes in the development paradigm but the necessity of a guiding hand can not be ignored altogether. The Indian experience of CDs has been very mixed till now. It probably indicates that the money market players have not fully realised its potential. There seems to be a mismatch in the purpose of demand and purpose of supply. On the demand side it is perceived as a profitable investment with a risk slightly more than that associated with government securities. On the supply side it is considered as a hedging instrument and not a profit earning instrument. The problem may lie with the reconciliation of these two intentions rather than with the instruments. The rift between the demand side and the supply side would keep on increasing unless this gap is bridged. With the continuous emphasis on availability of different opportunities to diversify the money market operations for its full development, delegating CDs to an early death solely due to a policy of non-interference seems contrary. The fact that this instrument is not in use or is not very popular in the major money markets of the world should not be given too much weightage. Indian experience in several fields has shown that a policy which has been found useful in developed countries does not always prove to be of equal benefit here. The western examples ought not to be emulated blindly. Even if they are done should India follow the US pattern where CDs are popular or that of London where they are not as popular? Thus the first option does not ensure a wise decision. The other money market instrument such as the Commercial Paper are not much older than CDs. Their performance might seem to be more consistent than that of CDs but the time period has been too short to establish the superiority of any other instrument over that of CDs. To take any step in favour of any other instrument so that it proves to be highly detrimental to CD at this juncture may not be wise.

Thus the second extreme alternative may not be advisable. Which leaves us with the third alternative. It is true that the direction of financial sector reforms do not advocate deep intervention by either the state or the RBI in the money market. Such a step would retract all the earlier efforts of the reforms. What can however be done is to undertake a quick but in depth study of the ups and downs displayed in the performance of CDs and then adopt the minimal regulatory changes to optimise the use of CDs. Some points for investigation could be explore how to make the CDs more profitable for the sellers. Would a reduction or a total abolition of stamp duty alter the administrative cost of CDs in their favor, compared to other types of deposits? The future trends in the money market are uncertain but with more freedom being given to the players in this market every day, it expected that it would cease to be as volatile as it had been in the past. The question to be investigated is whether a less volatile money market lead to a shift of investment to CDs from T-bills or Commercial Paper (which are more popular than CDs at present)? Another facet to be looked into is the extension of the money market from the centralized offices at Mumbai to other major trading centres such as Chennai, Calcutta or Ahmedabad. A few years ago the stock market operations were concentrated at Mumbai but have now spread over many centres. The Indian money market may also soon undergo this phenomenon. The corporations which are based in cities other than Mumbai would then find it easy to trade in CDs. Considering that CDs generally carry less risk than inter-corporate deposits, their usage may increase with the spread in money market operations to centres other than Mumbai. All the points mentioned above need further investigation.

References

Aftaion, F. and Bompaire, F. (1983); "France: Banking, Money and Bond Market" in George, AM and Giddy, IH (Eds) *International Finance Handbook*, Wiley Interscience Publication, New York, part 4.

Allen, D.L., (1983); "Japan: Banking, Money and Bond Market" in George, AM and Giddy, IH (Eds.) *op. cit.*

Auerbach, R.D. (1989); *Money Banking and Financial Markets*, Macmillan Publishing Co., New York, pp. 270-272.

Corti, M.A., (1983); "Switzerland: Banking, Money and Bond Market" in George, AM and Giddy, IH (Eds.) *op. cit.*

Dufey, G. and Krishnan, E. (1983); "West Germany: Banking, Money and Bond Market" in George, AM and Giddy, IH (Eds.). *op. cit.*

Handa, Rajiv (1995); "Certificate of Deposit on a Skyrocketing Trail," *Chartered Financial Analyst*, August, pp. 32-33.

Henning, C.N., Pigott, W., Scott, RH (1975); *Financial Markets and the Economy*, Prentice Hall Incorp., New Jersey, chap. 1.

IBA Bulletin, January 1997, back cover.

Jain, J.L. (1996); "Strategic Planning for Asset Liability Management" *The Journal of the Indian Institute of Bankers*, Oct.-Dec. p. 160.

Khan, M.Y. (1996); *Indian Financial System*, Tata McGraw Hill Publishing Co., New Delhi, pp. 6.20-6.22.

Reserve Bank of India Bulletin, February 1997.

Reserve Bank of India, *Credit Information Review*, No. 213, April 1997.

Vaghul, N. (1987); *Report of the Working Group on the Money Market*, Reserve Bank of India, Bombay.

Appendix A

Report of the Working Group on the Money Market, RBI 1987, Certificates of Deposit

(Page 29)

9.5 A Certificate of Deposit (CD) is a document of title to a time deposit. The CDs being bearer documents are readily negotiated and are attractive both to the banker and the investor in that the banker is not required to encash the deposit prematurely while the investor can sell the CD in the secondary market and thereby the instrument has ready liquidity.

9.6 In the Indian context, the Tambe Working Group in its Supplementary Report had made the following observations on CDs:

"there were divergent views among bankers in regard to the negotiable certificates of deposit (CD) as an alternative short-term instrument. One view was that the CDs could be introduced with the term and conditions to be worked out in consultation with the RBI and IBA. However, a majority of bankers doubted the wisdom of introduction of CDs on the grounds of its inherent weakness in the Indian context. The drawbacks specifically discussed were: (i) absence of secondary market, (ii) administered interest rate structure on bank deposits, and (iii) the danger of CDs giving rise to large number of fictitious transactions. On the basis of detailed discussion, the group came to the conclusion that. . . . Introduction of CDs with the shortcomings narrated above would not be advisable at this stage."

9.7 In view of the bulk nature of deposits (say not less than Rs. 10 crores), the Tambe Group was inclined to recommend placing short-term deposits (upto 180 days) with the scheduled commercial banks at an interest rate marginally higher (by one percent) than the corresponding rates on deposits of comparable maturities for the household sector.

9.8 The short-term deposit rates of banks continue to be very low and raising funds from institutions at rates only marginally higher than the banks present short-term deposit rates would be a feasible proposition. The Working Group is of the considered view that developing CDs as a money market instruments would not be meaningful unless the short-term deposit rates are aligned with other rates in the system. Accordingly, the Working Group does not recommend the introduction of CDs at this stage. The Working Group, however, recommends that in the context of the various changes proposed by the Working Group and the introduction of the 182 days Treasury Bill, the structure of short-term deposit rates upto one year as well as the number of maturities could be reviewed by the end of April 1987, and in the light of this review, the feasibility of introducing CDs could be reconsidered.

PART E

TRANSFORMATION OF INDIAN MONEY MARKET AND FURTHER REFORMS

11

Recent Changes in Money Market—Some Suggestions for Further Reforms

TULI ROY AND V. UPADHYAY

Money Market is market for short-term funds—generally up to one year. The assets in this market are liquid and are close substitutes for money which can be turned over quickly at low cost. The market facilitates adjustment of liquidity by the participants in the market. The different participants in a money market turn to this market for their liquidity management.[1] The money market operates through various instruments known as the money market instruments. Each instrument has its own characteristics, its problems and scope. Each instrument serves specific segments.

NEED FOR REFORMS

Prior to 1987 this Indian money market in the organised sector was a highly restricted market with a very narrow base. Entry into the market was limited and there were limited number of participants. There were no big traders to lend depth to the market and there was a paucity of instruments. The Sukhomoy Chakarvarty Committee 1985, had advocated that a well-developed money market would in itself be an important regulation measure. So in 1986 a working group headed by Shri N. Vaghul was set up to make a comprehensive review to money market and submit specific recommendation for its development. The Working Group submitted that the money market should provide an equilibrating mechanism for evening out short-term surplus and deficits, should provide a focal point for Central Bank intervention for influencing liquidity in the economy and provide a reasonable access to users of short-term money to meet their requirements at a realistic price.[2]

The recommendations of the Group were accepted by the Reserve Bank and changes were slowly brought in stages. A number of changes and measures were taken by the Reserve Bank to widen and deeper to market. These changess can be classified under two heads:

(a) Changes in money market instruments and
(b) Institutional building.

The various money market instruments in India are:

(1) Certificates of Deposit;
(2) Commercial Papers;
(3) Derivative Usance Pomissory Notes;
(4) Inter Bank Participation Certificates;
(5) Money Market Mutual funds;
(6) 14 days Treasury Bills;
(7) 91 days Treasury Bills;
(8) 182 days Treasury Bills;
(9) 364 days Treasury Bills.

CERTIFICATES OF DEPOSITS OR CDs

They were introduced into the market in June 1989. This was a major step forward in the deregulation of interest rates in deposits as it provided an avenue to corporates for investment at better and market related rates. These certificates of deposits were used by banks to provide better rates of interest to their more valued clients. The certificates of deposit have become very popular with all banks. In order to enable banks to raise more resources at competitive rates of interest, changes have been brought about by the Reserve Bank of India. From October 16, 1993 banks were given the freedom to issue CDs depending on their requirements. The outstanding CDs were Rs. 11,964 Crores as on April 25, 1997. However there is not much activity for CDs in the secondary market.

COMMERCIAL PAPERS

In March 1989, R.B.I. introduced the scheme of commercial papers which came into existence with effect from 01.01.1990. Commercial Papers or CPs as they are popularly known are unsecured short-term debt instruments of companies. They are issued in the form of negotiable promissory notes and provide an avenue for investment of short-term surpluses of companies, investors etc. with assured liquidity and risk which is linked to the company issuing the CPs. Various rules had been laid down by RBI for the issue of CPs to ensure that only very sound companies issue the papers. This paper allows the company to approach the investor directly for their short-term requirements. RBI has been making constant efforts to make the idea of CPs popular and thereby make them acceptable in the money market. Regulations were relaxed to allow small companies to issue CPs and this paper was also freed from the cash credit component in 1995-96, thus removing a major constraining factor in the CP issue. The total outstanding of companies as on May 31, 1997 is Rs. 1049.50 Crores. However the secondary market for CPs continue to remain dull as the investors prefer to hold on to them till maturity.

DERIVATIVE USANCE PROMISSORY NOTES (DUP_S)

The derivative usance promissory notes are issued upto a face value equal to the total amount of eligible bills held by the bank. The notes are transferable by endorsement and delivery. The operation of bill rediscounting scheme takes place through the DUPs as they are based on eligible bills. The

Discount and Finance House of Indian is the market maker for these bills but now the activity in these notes have slowed down very much. The scheme is yet to realise its full potential and will probably mature in the years to come.

INTER-BANK PARTICIPATION CERTIFICATES

Following the Vaghul Committee recommendations RBI announced the decision to introduce Inter Bank Participation in 1988. This is basically the participation of one bank in the assets of another bank. A bank can thus sell a portion of its assets to another bank for a consideration. These participation can be "with risk" and "without risk". "With risk" participation helps a bank to clear up its balance sheet and helps in adhering to the adequacy ratio. Recently there has been some activity in these certificates as the selling banks want to dress up their balance sheets by removing a portion of their NPAs. The buying banker participates as it improves its C-D ratio. However a major drawback is that they are not transferable and this restricts its liquidity. Not much data is available regarding participation but a general estimate is that there are not too many participation in the market.

MONEY MARKET MUTUAL FUNDS

In April 1991, RBI announced the introduction of money market mutual funds. It stated that "with a view to providing an additional short-term avenue to investors and to bring money market instruments within the reach of individuals and small bodies, it may be desirable to allow scheduled commercial banks and their subsidiaries to set up money market mutual funds". The main objectives of the money market mutual funds or MMMFs are to provide small investors another short-term investing opportunity yielding market related returns, help in broad basing money market by providing more participants and help in mobilising liquid household savings into production channels.[3] This will improve cash management of individuals. To give further impetus for growth of this innovative product, the private sector was allowed to set up MMMFs in November 1995, and the size and limits on investments by them were deregulated. In April 1996, corporates were also allowed to invest and finally, from July 1996 the minimum lock—in period was reduced from 46 days to 30 days. UTI, IDBI, Mutual fund, ABN Amro Bank and Bank of Madura Ltd. have been given clearance to set up MMMFs. Most of the irritants have been removed from the path of growth of this instrument but some do remain. The minimum lock-in period is one such irritant. This is new product and special marketing efforts are required to create awareness so that investors are induced to invest. MMMFs should also have proper infrastructure to provide a high standard of service to investors.

TREASURY BILLS

14-days Treasury Bills

Treasury Bill is an instrument of short-term borrowing of the Central Government. These 14 days Treasury Bills of TBs are the latest instruments in the money market. They were introduced into the money market by RBI in June 1997 and on June 6, 1997 the first auction of these bills were held. This move has been welcomed by the money market players as it filled a long-felt need. Since 91 days treasury bills were the minimum maturity available, banks had very few options for periods less than 91-days. Call money was the other option but it was for not more than two or three days. "The new paper will complete the yield curve" says a primary dealer. Since the 14-day TBs will be issued every week, traders expect the yield rates will be between call rates and the yield on 91-days treasury bills. Secondly, since the 14-day TBs will be issued every week, it will serve as a very short-term paper for investors who required this kind of maturity. In the first auction held on June 6, 1997, RBI accepted bids worth Rs. 1114 Crores while Rs. 160 Crores devolved on the primary dealers. However a major weakness of this instrument is that it is not eligible for repo facility. There is also the possibility that these TBs may drive the 91-day TBs out of the market, just as the introduction of 364-day TBs made 182-day TBs redundant.[4]

91-days Treasury Bills

Initially there were only 91-day tap TBs. In November 1986,

182-day TBs were introduced and after that came the 364-day TBs and now the 14-day TBs. Till 1992, 91-day TBs were available on tap from the counters of RBI at a discount of 4.6%. This discount had not changed since July 23, 1974 and Sukhomoy Chakravarty Committee had recommended that these bills should provide a yield which is at least marginally positive in real terms. In 1992-93, RBI pursued an active debt management policy to prudently influence the composition, maturity structure and yield of government securities and thus many reform measures were introduced like auction of 364-day & 91-day TBs. At present the yields of 91-day TBs are significantly higher (ranging between 12.4% and 7.2% during May '96 to April '97) than the earlier fixed discount rate of 4.6% per annum. State Government and non-government provident funds were allowed to participate in the auction of these TBs on a non-competitive basic from July 1994.

182-Days Treasury Bills

Government of India introduced these TBs in November 1986. The recommendations of the Sukhomoy Chakarvarty Committee were accepted and monthly auctions were started. This periodicity changed to fortnightly auctions in July 1988. However with the introduction of 364-day TBs giving higher yield than 182-day TBs, the issue of the 182-day TB was discontinued.

364-Days Treasury Bills

Treasury bills gained further prominence since April 1992 when the auction of 364-day TBs was introduced. These bills gave a higher yield which were closely aligned to the market related rates. They were as high as 12.96% in June '96 before falling to 8.9% in May '97. Funding of these TBs are an important aspect of internal debt management. However to provide more depth to this market, Foreign Institutional Investors may be allowed to invest.

Institutional Building

The players in the primary money market need a good, well-developed secondary market. Thus in the past few years a lot of attention has been given to build a strong institutional structure which will develop a secondary market with players with different perceptions which will impart an element of liquidity in the market.

DFHI—The Discount and Finance House of India (DFHI) was set up in January 1988, jointly by the Reserve Bank, public sector banks and the All India Financial Institutions to deal in short-term money market instruments, enlarge the number of participants in the call, short notice and term money market by allowing financial institutions and mutual funds to participate as lenders. It has been endeavouring to moderate the volatility in the inter-bank call money market by providing liquidity in the market as and when it was required. However some slow down in its activity has been noticed in the past couple of years.

STCI—The Securities Trading Corporation of India set up on June 7, 1994 to develop an institutional infrastructure to act as base for an active secondary market in government dated securities and public sector bonds. It can also hold short-term money market assets like TBs as part of its liquidity management.

The other developments in building a good institutional infrastructure are the GOI and RBI agreed in 1994 to limit the net issue adhoc TBs to Rs. 6000 Crores. The excessively large borrowing program of the government was blunting the open-market operations of RBI, so on March 31, 1997 the adhoc TBs at Rs. 34,130 Crores were converted into special securities without any specified maturity at an interest rate of 4.6% per annum on April 1, 1997. Thus the system of issue of adhocs was totally discontinued from April 1, 1997 and was replaced by Ways and Means Advances.[5] However a fear is that raising debt at market related rates by the government will lead to a rise in the interest rates, raising the costs in the economy.

To create more transparency and disseminate information, particulars of transactions in Government securities put through SGL accounts at RBI Mumbai were released to the Press daily from September 1, 1994. On March 29, 1995 RBI issued guidelines and procedures for enlistment of Primary Dealers in Government securities market, and six primary dealers (PDs) have been set up. The PDs are also allowed access to commercial paper market to help develop the secondary market. "In principle" approval has been given for satellite dealers. The progressive movement towards a mark to market system for valuation of government securities has resulted in greater trading in securities and imparted more depth to the market.

Remaining Lacunae

Although a lot of changes have taken place, Indian money market is yet to attain maturity. There are procedural hassles and high transaction costs. Procedures are not simplified and restrictions continue to remain. SGL accounts are not available to corporates, brokers and FIIs so it raises their transactions costs in cases where they transact in government securities. Auction of government securities are held only in Mumbai and this restricts the area of operation. House-hold saving have been neglected for a long time and they need to be tapped. Bill Rediscounting Scheme has slowed down because the initial incentives given by RBI are no longer present. This market needs to be revived. Though the CPs and CDs have a good primary market, the secondary market continues to be subdued as the investors prefer to hold on to the papers till maturity.

SUGGESTIONS

The stamp duty on CPs and CDs need to be removed as this is hindering the development of a good secondary market for the papers. Removal of stamp duty will bring down transactions costs and simplify procedures.

Money Market Mutual funds need to be well-marketed and there should be greater transparency in explaining the instrument to the investors, as this instrument can tap the hitherto neglected household sector. The minimum lock in period should be done away with altogether.

There should be greater transparency in publishing information and closer links need to be brought about between money, capital and gilt edged markets. Corporates and FIIs may be allowed to open SGL account. Foreign Institutional Investors have been allowed and invest in Central and State government dated papers. They may be allowed to invest in treasury bills also.

- — The scope of satellite dealers can be increased.
- — Foreign currency money market instruments can be introduced in India as this will bring about greater integration between the foreign exchange market and money market, since now we are talking about capital account convertibility.
- — Repo facility may introduced for 14-day treasury bills.
- — Auction of government securities can be held at least in the four metros to widen the scope and area of operation.
- — There is also a greater need to increase the number of participants in the market. While the number of instruments have increased, the base of investors have not increased much correspondingly. More players in the market will widen the market. The market needs less regulations and restriction which will help facilitate ease of transactions. More formalised, simplified and accepted procedures will help serve the market better.

Notes and References

1. Karnik, A.G., *Macro Economic Policy and Money Market.*
2. Vaghul Committee Report (1987), Report of the Working Group on the Money Market.
3. Sengupta, A.K. and Agarwal, M.K. (1994), *Money Market Operations in India.*
4. *Business Standard,* dated 12.06.97.
5. *RBI Press Release* on 3rd April' 1997.
6. *RBI Newsletter,* Vol. 22 May 15, 1996, No. 9.
7. *Report on Trend and Progress of Banking in India* 1992-96.

12

Emerging Money Market in India: Agenda for Further Reforms

B.K. Bhoi

INTRODUCTION

A systematic review of India's money market was undertaken by the Vaghul Working Group in 1987. Since then, quite a number of steps have been taken to improve the efficiency of the Indian money market. Moreover, the operating environment today is considerably different from the same a decade ago, mainly because of wide ranging financial sector reforms which have been put in place based on the Narasimham Committee Report (1991). Hence, there is a need to take a relook, at this stage, as to whether Indian money market has achieved efficiency as visualised by the Vaghul Working Group. If not, then what rae the major weaknesses which persist today? What could be the basic reasons for the persistence of several pitfalls? An attempt has been made here to critically examine the major weaknesses of Indian money market that are still persisting and suggest some remedial measures.

The scheme of this paper is as follows: Section I presents

an overview of Indian money market, highlights the desirable objectives and identifies the major weaknesses. Section II explains the general environment in which the Indian money market operates. Section III deals with issues specific to each segment of the money market. Section IV briefly comments on the developments in the Government securities market as it is considered as an integral part of the money market. Section V offers a few suggestions which are discernible from the examination of various segmets of the money market. The extent guidelines currently in vogue with respect to each segment of money market are presumed to be known to the players and therefore, discussion is limited to the major issues.

I. AN OVERVIEW OF INDIAN MONEY MARKET

Money market in India is currently at a crucial stage of evolution. The operation of Indian money market is no more limited to inter-bank transactions. Participants are fairly large notwithstanding restrictions on certain institutions in the mode of their participation. Moreover, quite a number of instruments are also available which include call/notice/term money, Commercial Papers (CPs), Certificates of Deposit (CDs), Participation Certificates (PCs), commercial bills and Government papers including dated government securities. Of late, measures have been taken to introduce Money Market Mutual Funds (MMMF). Each instrument has a separate market of its own. The institutions, instruments and markets relating to money market in India are shown in Exhibit I. The operating procedures are changing from time to time depending on the changing environment. Exhibit 2 gives the major reforms in the Indian Money Market.

The desirable objectives of money market reforms in India are : (1) to integrate all the segments; (b) to develop secondary market for each instrument; (c) to improve turnover of each instrument in primary as well as in secondary markets; (d) to reduce volatility of interest rates; and (e) to provide a focal point for central bank intervention for the transmission of monetary policy.

EXHIBIT 1

Money Market in India

Institutions	*Instruments*	*Markets*
-RBI	-Money (Call, Notice)	-Call Money Market
-DFHI/STCI	-Treasury Bills	-Treasury Bills Market
-Banks	-Govt. Securities	-Govt. Securities Market
-Financial Institutions	-Trade Bills	- Bills Discounting Market
- Mutual Funds	-Commercial Papers	-CP Market
-Non-Bank Financial Companies	-Certificates of Deposits	-CD Market
-MMMF	-Collateral Loans	- Loan Market
-Primary Dealers	-Repos	- Repos Market
-Others	-Participation Certificate	-PC Market

EXHIBIT 2

Major Reforms in Indian Money Market

Since Vaghul Working Group has submitted their Report in 1987, the following reforms in Indian Money Market have been undertaken:

1. Ceiling on call money rate imposed by the Indian Bank Association (IBA) has been withdrawn since May 1989.
2. A number of institutions have been set up like DFHI, STCI and Primary/Satellite Dealers to promote the orderly development of money market. They are allowed to participate both as lenders and borrowers in the call money market.
3. The base of call money market has been widened by selective increase in the participants as lenders (Appendix 1).
4. Selected institutions are also allowed to borrow from the money market on a term basis.
5. Certificates of Deposit is introduced in 1989 and guidelines relating to it have been modified from time to time.

6. Commercial Papers have been introduced since 1990 and guidelines relating to CPs have been changed from time to time.
7. Interest rate on all money market instruments are market determined.
8. Guidelines have been issued in April 1992 to set up MMMFs and they are revised from time to time.
9. A number of reforms relating to Government securities have been implemented as given in Appendix 2.
10. CRR and SLR on inter bank liabilities were removed subject to the condition that effective CRR and SLR maintained by scheduled commercial banks on total demand and time liabilities should not be less than 3 per cent and 25 per ent, respectively.
11. To further develop money market and make it more efficient, a Standing Advisory Committee on Money Market (Chairman: Dr. Y.V. Reddy) was set up on April 28, 1997 to advise the Reserve Bank.

Major weaknesses of the Indian money market are the following:

(a) Indian money market is yet to acquire depth. Despite a number of reform measures which have been taken during the last decade, the volume of transaction remains abysmally low (in primary as well as in secondary markets) in case of the most of the instruments except call money and to some extent, in Government papers. Despite setting up of a few specialised institutions like Discount and Finance House of India (DFHI), Security Trading Corporation of India (STCI), Primary Dealers, the volume of transactions is unimpressive in the money market;
(b) The gyration in the interest rate/returns is sometimes woefully high;
(c) The markets corresponding to each instrument are segmented although signs of integration among various segments are visible during the recent years;
(d) The term money market is yet to develop in India

and therefore no reference rate is available; and

(e) The money market is yet to acquire desired level of efficiency to transmit the monetary policy impulses to the real sector at a reasonably good speed.

II. GENERAL ENVIRONMENT

Money market is essentially an integral part of the whole financial system. Hence, money market operation in India needs to be understood in the context of the working of the whole financial system of the country. Based on the Vaghul Working Group Report (1987), interest rates were first deregulated in the money market when they were under control in the rest of the financial system. Hence, it is but natural for the money market, especially the call money market, to bear the burden of equilibrating between demand for and supply of funds in the financial system. This point needs a little more elaboration. According to the Reserve Bank guidelines, commercial banks are supposed to meet statutory obligations as a first charge on their deposit resources. Being guided by the profit motive, commercial banks generally do the opposite. They deploy the resources first and then they search for funds for reserve requirements later. If the credit market is tight, then money market, especially the call money market, turns tight and *vice versa*. Similarly, conditions prevailing in capital market may also cast their shadows on the credit market which may be ultimately reflected in the money market. The origin of volatility in the money market rates, therefore, could be traced to the conditions prevailing in several other segements of the financial system.

Deregulation of the financial sector in India is incomplete. Going by the international experience, most of the countries adopt a cautious approach with respect to financial sector reform so as to avoid adverse affects on savings and/or investment and ultimately on the overall growth of the economy. On the basis of the Narasimham Committee recommendations, financial sector reforms in India have been gradual. Nevertheless, structural reforms are probably faster in the financial sector than those in the real sector. Even today, the agenda in respect of financial sector reforms, which remains unfinished, include, *inter alia*, directed credit, high CRR, administered structure of interest rate in certain segments, sector specific refinance (export credit) and above all, complicated credit delivery system. Moreover, the non-bank intermediaries, currently engaged in the mobilisation of public savings and deployment of funds, have assumed significant proportion. Their transactions are non-transparent and rates are generally high. Unless financial sector reforms are complete, it would be difficult for complete integration of the financial markets. In this context, the reforms of the payment system also assumes significance. Aymmetry in the information system and delay in the settlement of payments may provide arbitrage opportunities and thereby cause distortion in the transmission mechanism.

In most of the developed countries, money market instruments are first innovated by the banks/marketing agencies. The proliferations of the money market innovations in those countries remain generally unnoticed until they interfere with the regulatory mechanism. By the time they are targetted for integration into the regulatory system, their size of operation might have become fairly large. *Per contra*, most of the money market instruments in India are introduced by the regulatory authorities. It is but natural for the authorities to be extra-cautious about the ramifications of their introduction and therefore, several conditions are attached at the early stage of the introduction of each instrument. Given the guidelines, the marketing agencies should find them worthwhile to introduce. Unless, it is commercialy viable and profitable to both the parties, the size of operation may not pick up. It is generally felt that the environment is not congenial for the growth of certain money market instruments within the regulatory framework.

III. SEGMENT-SPECIFIC ISSUES

In addition to the observations made in the previous Section, issues peculiar to each segment of the money market will be dealt with in this Section.

Call Money Market

At the early stage of the liberalisation, call money rates were extremely volatile (Bhoi, 1993a). By and large, the degree of volatility is on the decline over the years. Nevertheless, going by international standards, fluctuations in call money rates in India are fairly high. With a view to augmenting the lendable resources, permission has been given, on a selective basis, to a number of institutions to participate in the call money market as lenders (Appendix I). In spite of this measure, Indian money market, more particularly the call money market, is characterised by hard instinct. There is near-panic situation when SBI, one of the major lenders in the call money market, turns borrower for some reason or other.

In most of the advanced countries, call rates are range bound and there are mechanisms to bring the call rates to equilibrium within a short period. In sharp contrast, variations in the call rates in India are erratic. It is true that Reserve Bank's money market interventions through DFHI and STCI have mellowed down call rates on several occasions but *could not make them range bound.*

Moreover, simultaneous intervention in call money market and forex market may not be desirable in Indian condition as the purpose of intervention in either market is likely to be defeated. For example, a tight money market may encourage the authorised dealers (ADs), in the first lag, to generate rupee resources by selling foreign exchange, say US dollar. In the second lag, when the ADs go for forward cover, the forward premia may shoot up. In the post liberalisation period, the correlation between call rate and forward premia of the US dollar has been found to be positive and significant. In view of this, intervention in both the markets may offset the level of primary liquidity in the market and thereby neither prevent a precipitate fall in the external value of rupee nor bring down the call rate. When call money market and forex market are being integrated, interventions in either market need to be synchronised in a manner such that distortion is minimised.

Of late, Reserve Bank has been using a new instrument called *repos* to mop up excess liquidity from the money market particularly when the call market is extremely easy. The timing of *repos* generally coincide with reporting Fridays. Of late, short-term *repos* (3-4 days) are being conducted for liquidity management. In course of time, *repo* rate may emerge as the *floor rate* for call money market. In order for the ceiling rate to emerge, there is probably a need for rediscounting of bills/

Government papers, (may be) at a penal rate. This may be possible when RBI credit to Central Government is minimum and Reserve Bank has enough elbow room to conduct its monetary policy. To begin with, reverse *repos* may be used to set the *ceiling rate* in the call money market. This is similar to the German model of money market operation where call rates remain range bound between discount rate and Lombard rate (*Bhoi* 1993b).

Term Money Market

Term money market is virtually absent in India. It did not grow mainly because of administered structure of interest rate, rationing of credit and sector specific refinance. Despite wide ranging financial sector reforms undertaken during the recent years, several hurdles still persist. Discussed below are some of the major factors which have been acting as impediments to the growth of the term money market in India.

The statutory Cash Reserve Ratio (CRR) on inter-bank liabilities was considered as the major hurdle in the process of the development of term money market. Expert-Group on foreign exchange market (headed by O.P. Sodhani, 1995) has also recommended that inter-bank liabilities should be excluded from the NDTL so that term money market would develop. Monetary authorities have accepted this suggestion with effect from April 26, 1997 subject to the minimum stipulation of CRR & SLR at 3 per cent and 25 per cent, respectively of the total demand and time liabilities including inter-bank borrowing. However, the term money market is yet to pick up.

One of the major factors responsible for the tardy growth of term money market in India is *uncertainty* about the interest rate which has been found to be highly erratic in the short-end of the market in the deregulated regime. As the deregulation is incomplete, the dust is yet to settle with respect to interest rate, although interest rate volatility has been reduced considerably during the recent period.

Secondly, there are attractive avenues for the deployment of surplus funds on a short-term basis. Currently, several Government papers of varying maturities are available both in the primary and secondary markets. Moreover, banks can also generate short-term resources through inter-bank repurchase agreement (Repos) against Treasury bills and select dated securities. This apart, Reserve Bank also conducts repos when market is extremely easy. Other than Government papers, security based transactions could be undertaken on Commercial Papers, Certificates of Deposit and PSU Bonds. When better opportunities like secured transactions, sometimes with repurchase option, are available, banks generally do not prefer unsecured term money transactions, particularly when there is a good deal of uncertainty about the interest rate on an *ex ante* basis.

Thirdly, the asset profiles of the commercial banks cannot be accurately anticipated in advance as sizeable portion of the credit needs of the corporate sector is met through cash credit system. Term borrowing/lending is considered imprudent by the banks as the cash flows are unpredictable under cash credit system. On the contrary, had the requirements of corporate clients been met largely by a system of bill rediscounting or loan system, cash flow of the banks might have been anticipated more accurately. Unless commercial banks have definite short-term asset/liability structure, there would be no incentive for term lending/borrowing to match the assets and liabilities.

Fourthly, commercial banks have some short-term assets in their portfolio like, export credits which are relatively more definite. The resources for export credit have been made available by Reserve Bank through export credit refinance on an ongoing basis. Hence, there is no need for term borrowing from the market. Until recently, adequate refinance was available for the banks to support the directed credit. Recently, however, there is a move towards phasing out of sector specific refinance. So long as refinance facility is available in sizeable amount, term money market will not gather momentum.

Money Market Mutual Funds (MMMFs)

In India, Money Market Mutual Funds (MMMFs) are yet to pick up despite the fact that Reserve Bank had issued guidelines in April 1992 and revised them in November 1995. The scheme was made more attractive to investors by reducing the lock-in period from 46 days to 30 days effective July 3, 1996. The scheme was made more flexible by bringing it on par with all other mutual funds by allowing them to invest in rated corporate bonds and debentures with a residual maturity up to one year.

One of the major reasons behind the failure on the part of the financial institutions and banks to introduce MMMFs is that a reasonable spread (between cost of funds and average return on the money market instruments) is not available. For example, it is difficult on the part of the MMMFs to mobilise funds unless they offer a return close to the rates offered by the existing mutual funds. The typical interest rate offered by existing mutual funds would be around 13 per per cent for one year maturity which is higher than the deposit rate. As MMMFs have to mobilise short-term funds, they have to offer somewhere between deposit rate and mutual funds rate, say, about 10-12 per cent. An operating spread of about 2 per cent over the cost of funds is probably the minimum requirement for any fund to remain in business. Given the money market conditions, an average return of about 12 to 14 per cent or above is probably not feasible and hence banks are reluctant to show any enthusiasm to introduce MMMFs.

Needless to say that the cost of funds should be low so that a reasonable spread is available. Unless deposit rates in the banks and those offered by the existing mutual funds are reduced, there is little chance for MMMFs to be profitable. Banks and mutual funds also face competition as the prevailing interest rates in the non-bank intermediaries continue to remain higher than those offered by these institutions. The operating environment is, thus, not attractive for the setting up of MMMFs.

Commercial Papers

Commercial papers have never been an avenue to mobilise additional resources for the corporate sector. It has been tagged to Maximum Permissible Bank Finance (MPBF) in some form or the other. Although the system of MPBF has been withdrawn, the issue of CP would continue to be within the fund-based working capital limit. The major problem of commercial papers is that their volume has never exceeded 2 per cent of the total non-food credit although enterprises, which fulfill certain requirements, are allowed to finance up to 100 per cent of their working capital requirement. The transactions in the secondary market is negligible as the holders prefer to hold till its maturity because of attractive return. Moreover, as the commercial banks are the major subscriber to the CPs, the amount outstanding increases when money market, more particularly the call money market, is easy and declines when money market turns tight. Although banks were allowed to subscribe to CPs, the spirit of introducing CPs was that the corporate entities with surplus funds should subscribe to the CPs floated by the deficient corporate units. As the inter-corporate deposit rates ruled generally high, surplus entities in the corporate sector did not subscribe to the CPs in a big way unless the CP rates are higher than the inter-corporate deposit rates.

When safeguards for the banks are being ensured through prudential regulations, rationing of credit may not be necessary except for a short period during transition. In this context, the concept of Maximum Permission Bank Finance has partly lost its relevance. In view of this, commercial papers may be allowed as an additional source of financing. As a prudential regulation, the commercial banks may be allowed to subscribe to the CPs at PLR or above. This is likely to put pressure on the banks to reduce PLR. There should be no bar for the cash rich companies to subscribe to CPs at rates below PLR.

One of the major hurdles for the growth of CP market is that there is a lock-in period of 30 days during which holder cannot dispose them in the secondary market. This restriction has been retained as there was corresponding regulation with respect to deposit rate. As interest rate on term deposit rate has been completely deregulated, there exists a case to reduce the lock-in period with respect to CPs and CDs. To begin with, the lock-in period for CDs and CPs may be reduced to 15 days so that it will promote the growth of secondary market in CDs and CPs.

Certificates of Deposit (CDs)

The amount outstanding in CDs and CPs move almost like a sea-saw. If money market is tight, then CPs will shrink and the commercial banks, being the major subscribers, reduce their commitment to CPs. On the other hand, commercial banks find it worthwhile to mobilise funds through CDs by paying a little more than the deposit rates if immediate returns from the money market are high. When money market is easy, commercial banks reduce the amount outstanding in high cost CDs as a part of prudent liquidity management. As the CD rates are attractive, the holders generally do not like to dispose them in the secondary market. Moreover, the minimum lock-in period of 30 days acts as an obstacle to the growth of secondary market in CDs.

If we carefully examine the conditions attached to the issue of CPs, CDs, MMMF, they are found to be initially unattractive for the parties involved to introduce them. The prevailing environment may be equally unrewarding for the expansion of the business. For example, the size of the CP market is limited by the cash credit system which is more attractive to the corporate sector as the burden of liability management squarely falls on the banks. Only when market rate, more particularly call rate is substantially low, banks finance corporate sector through CP route. The return on CPs are generally very attractive and therefore, holders prefer to hold it till maturity.

IV. DEVELOPMENT OF GOVERNMENT SECURITY MARKET

In the context of the money market developments, the Government securities occupy a crucial place. The Treasury bills of all maturities and Government dated securities with unexpired maturities up to one year are strictly treated as money market instruments. However, Government securities with unexpired maturities above one year are also used in case of short-term repo transactions. Outright sales and purchases of Government securities under Open Market Operations by the RBI do influence money market activities. Moreover, Government has also introduced new instruments such as zero coupon bonds, partly paid stocks, tap issue of Government securities. Although these are fairly medium term securities, they are eligible for repo transactions.

Development of government securities market is fundamental to the smooth working of both money and capital markets. The government papers, in fact, provide a bench mark for returns on other instruments and also act as the link between money and capital markets. A number of measures have been taken during the recent years to develop the secondary market in government securities (Appendix 2). As a logical first step, Government has taken the conscious decision to move to market related rates of interest in respect of its borrowing programme. The Government has also phased out since April, 1997 the automatic monetisation of budget deficit through *ad hoc* Treasury bills. A separate mechanism under the Ways and Means Advance has been formalised. The 'Primary Dealers' System now in force would become fully operational over time and absorb the unsubscribed portion of Government loans. Development of Government Securities on RBI would be eliminated in due course. Moreover, Delivery Versus Payment (DVP) System has been introduced to speed up the process of settlement and avert counter-party risk.

Despite several measures, the magnitude of SGL transactions in Government Securities has been low. The Central Bank should increase the size of its operations in Government Securities for the day-to-day liquidity management. Once, the GFD is reasonably low and the extent of monetisation is minimum, the Central Bank may have enough flexibility in controlling liquidity without jeopardising its objective of price stability. Ultimately what is needed is to diversify the holding of Government securities. Primary dealers as well as commercial banks should promote retailing of Government securities so that holdings of government papers can be diversified.

V. SUGGESTIONS

On the basis of the discussions made in the previous sections, a few suggestions relevant to the development of money market in India at this moment are enumerated below:

1. There should be a mechanism to make the call rate range bound whih may reduce uncertainty and provide confidence to the bankers for term lending/borrowing. In this context, it is emphasised that Repos and Reverse Repos conducted by RBI has the potential to set the *floor* and *ceiling* in the call money market respectively. If the participants can fairly anticipate, on an *ex ante* basis, the corridor within which call rate can fluctuate, they may be encouraged to participate in the term money market.

2. Repos and reverse repos may not always be sufficient to set the floor and ceiling of the call money market. Therefore, repo mechanism needs to be supplemented by Open Market Operation (OMO). Besides sending interest rate signals to the market, OMO can influence the volume of liquidity as well. In this context, a collateral borrowing window may be useful with interest rate left to the discretion of the monetary authority.

3. Over a period of time, Cash Reserve Ratio (CRR) can be brought down to the statutory minimum of 3 per cent in a phased manner. Currently, there is a move towards universal banking. Therefore, there is a need for level playing field. To begin with, all non-bank financial intermediaries be subjected to minimum statutory stipulations for the short-term deposits mobilised by them.

4. Penalty on CRR default was set at 25 per cent when lending rate was around 20 per cent. As lending rate has come down considerably, penalty on account of CRR default could be reduced, say, from 25 per cent to 20 per cent. Ultimately, CRR default could be related to Bank Rate, say, Bank Rate plus 5 per cent.

5. As far as practicable, exchange rate should be market determined. Intervention, if necessary, should be made in the forward market. Spot market intervention should be made sparingly, only if exchange rate is highly misaligned. Intervention in the forex market needs to be synchronised with money market intervention.

6. Commercial banks have to improve their information system so that asset and liability management is improved. Fund management, treasury management and forex operation within the commercial banks should be integrated.

7. Cash credit system should be phased out so that banks should be in a better position to manage their cash flows. The asset/liabilities mismatches could then be met from the term money market.

8. Sector specific refinance needs to be completely withdrawn. Currently, only export credit refinance is in vogue which is also not used to its limit by the commercial banks because liquidity condition is comfortable. In case of stringency, there can be variable rate rediscounting of export bills to tide

over the situation rather than to continue with export credit refinance as it is partly acting as impediment to the growth of term money market in India.

9. Transparency should be ensured in money market transactions. There should be screen based trading with two way quotas for each money market instruments. Deals may be settled on a real time basis.

10. The lock-in period for CDs and CPs may be initially reduced to 15 days and completely withdrawn at an opportune time.

11. Corporates may be allowed to float CPs as an additional channel of financing their working capital requirements. As a safeguard against the misuse of bank funds, commercial banks should be allowed to subscribe to CPs not below the PLR. The CP rate may be market determined for all non-bank subscribers including cash-rich companies.

12. Money Market Mutual Funds should be set up by the commercial banks and other financial institutions. The lock-in period of funds may be waived. As MMMF would be investing on money market instruments which are short term in nature, there may not be cash flow problem in case of heavy withdrawals.

13. Retailing of government papers should be encouraged. In this context, the Primary Dealers can play a constructive role as market makers. If necessary, incentive may be given for the transactions in the clients' accounts.

14. Currently, Foreign Institutional Investors are allowed to participate in the primary as well as secondary markets for Government dated securities. They may be allowed to transact on 91 Days Treasury bills as well.

15. Non-bank segment should be brought under same regulation on par with Banks as early as possible so that level playing field can be established. To begin with, companies which have not registered with RBI as per recent regulation, should not be allowed to mobilise public deposits beyond their net owned funds.

16. There is a need to promote the growth of bill market and the market for Participation Certificates. While the former is dormant, the latter is virtually non-existent in India. Legal

framework may be tightened against accommodation bills of the kite flying parties.

References

Bhoi, B.K. (1993a), "Analytics of the Recent Call Money Rate Behaviour in India", *RBI Occasional Papers*, Vol. 14 No. 4 December.

——— (1993b), "Money Market Operations and Liquidity Management in the UK and Germany, RBI Staff Studies, No. SS (DEAP): 7/93.

Reserve Bank of India (1987), *Report of the Working Group of the Money Market* (Chairman, N. Vaghul).

——— (1991): Report of the Committee on the Financial System (Chairman, M. Narasimham).

——— (1995), Report of the Expert Group on Foreign Exchange Markets in India (Chairman, O.P. Sodhani).

APPENDIX 1

List of Institutions Permitted to Participate in the Call/ Notice Money Market

(A) Permitted to Operate both as Lenders and Borrowers

1. All Scheduled Commercial Banks
2. Co-operative Banks
3. Discount and Finance House of India Ltd.
4. Securities Trading Corporation of India Ltd.
5. Primary Dealers

(B) Permitted to Operate as Lenders

1. Life Insurance Corporation of India
2. Unit Trust of India
3. General Insurance Corporation and its subsidiaries
4. Industrial Development Bank of India
5. National Bank for Agriculture and Rural Development
6. Industrial Credit and Investment Corporation of India Ltd.
7. Industrial Reconstruction Bank of India
8. Export Credit and Guarantee Corporation of India Ltd.
9. SBI Mutual Fund
10. Canbank Mutual Fund
11. Industrial Finance Corporation of India
12. National Housing Bank
13. Shipping Credit and Investment Company of India Ltd.
14. Tourism Finance Corporation of India Ltd.
15. Export Import Bank of India
16. LIC Mutual Fund
17. Small Industries Development Bank of India
18. BOI Mutual Fund
19. Indian Bank Mutual Fund
20. PNB Mutual Fund
21. GIC Mutual Fund
22. BOB Mutual Fund
23. IDBI Mutual Fund

24. Birla Mutual Fund
25. Morgan Stanley Mutual Fund
26. Apple Mutual Fund
27. Shriram Mutual Fund
28. J.M. Mutual Fund
29. Kothari Pioneer Mutual Fund
30. CRB Mutual Fund
31. ICICI Mutual Fund
32. Alliance Capital Mutual Fund
33. 20th Century Mutual Fund
34. Taurus Mutual Fund
35. Power Finance Corporation
36. Reliance Capital Mutual Fund
37. Tata Mutual Fund
38. Jardine Fleming Mutual Fund
39. H.B. Mutual Fund
40. Templeton Fund
41. Sund F and C. Mutual Fund
42. Escorts Mutual Fund.

APPENIX 2

Reforms in the Government Securities Market

1. Maturity period for new issues of Central Government securities shortened from 20 to 10 years. Maturity of State Government securities shortened from 15 to 10 years.
2. The system of switch quota for banks and financial institutions discontinued since April 1992.
3. The 364-day Treasury bills replaced 182-day Treasury bills 1992-93 and are sold by fortnightly auctions since April 1992.
4. Auction of 91-day Treasury bills commenced from January 1993.
5. Treasury bills of various maturities (such as, 14-day, 28-day) have been introduced.
6. Funding of auction Treasury bills into a fixed coupon dated security at the option of holders introduced since April 19, 1993.
7. State Government and eligible provident funds are allowed to participate in 91-day Treasury bills auctions on a non-competitive basis from August 1994.
8. Details of transactions in Government securities put through Subsidiary General Ledger (SGL) accounts being published since September 1994 to improve market transparency.
9. Five new instruments introduced: (a) Zero Coupon Bonds on January 18, 1994, (b) Tap-stock on July 29, 1994, (c) Partly-Paid Government Stock on November 15, 1994, (d) Another instrument, combining the features of tap stock and partly-paid stock on September 11, 1995, (e) Yet another new instrument of Floating Rate Bonds introduced on September 29, 1995.
10. System of Primary Dealers and Satellite Dealers in Government securities has become operational. PDs are allowed to issue CPs to mobilise short-term funds.
11. Funding of Treasury bills into a dated security introduced through the auction mechanism in April 1995.

12. A system of Delivery Versus Payment (DVP) in SGL transactions introduced at Bombay (July 1995).
13. Reverse repo facility with RBI in Government dated securities extended to Discount and Finance House of India (DFHI) and Securities Trading Corporation of India (STCI) to provide liquidity support to their operations to stabilise call money rate. The earlier refinance facility to these two institutions for such securities have been withdrawn. Refinance facility against Treasury bills, however, continued.
14. Foreign Institutional Investors are allowed to participate both in primary and secondary markets of Government dated securities.
15. Automatic monetisation of budget deficit through *ad hoc* Treasury bills discontinued w.e.f. April 1, 1997 and system of Ways and Means as Advance has been put in Place.
16. Various measures have been taken for retailing of the Government securities with non-bank clients.

13

Transformation of Indian Money Market—Which Way?

AMALESH BANERJEE, PRATUL CHATTERJEE

Indian money market is in a state of transformation. The direction and the degree of transformation will determine the nature of growth of the economy. There were two phases of reform; one on the line of recommendations done by expert committees before economic reform process were started in 1991 and, the second phase is the liberalisation policy now being perceived by the Government. In both these phases the main objective remained the same—to induct flexibility and competitiveness in the money market. But the structure of our economy is yet to change. The present paper wishes to identify the flow of fund in the money market and points out that all the changes are taking place in the urban money market to the neglect of real and also rural finance which is now the fast changing sector of our economy. In the part I we see the objectives and the nature of reforms undertaken. In the part II implications and limitations of the reform. In part III the nature of reform needed in money market for rural development. In part IV we draw the conclusions.

I. CHANGES IN INDIAN MONEY MARKET

Objectives: Indian money market is changing in respect of institutional structure, instruments, coverage and operations. Before going into all these dimensions of change we first see the underlying objectives of this transformation. The fundamental objective of the reform of Indian money market was to make it competitive and resilient at national and international market by reducing the control and command of the administration. In order to do that the institutions, instruments and the interest rate structure have to be overhauled so that efficient movement of fund in short-term and medium-term activities is possible at a reasonable cost. More particularly, the money market with widened base must serve as an equilibrium structure in which the surplus and deficit funds are adjusted and the Central Bank can effectively intervene to control the liquidity.

Theoretically the financial regression hypothesis has been arguing for a market oriented financial system so that financial deepening takes place without excessive control. Vaghul Committee (1987) and the Chakraborty Committee (1985) have suggested a number of strategies for that.[1] It was suggested, by the Vaghul Committee, that monetary base has to be developed in a wide scale, exchange float and the interest rate deregulation has to be started and the new institutions have to be developed for domestic and international mobility of fund.[2] The Chakraborty Committee has specificially suggested for developing the government treasury bill market on a competitive footing so that expenditure of the government may indirectly be regulated by the market forces. Following Mckinnon-Shaw,[3] hypothesis of financial deepening the Chakraborty Committee pointed out that given this liberalised deregulation of the money market and the interest rate the central bank can regulate the liquidity and set the target of monetary expansion consistent with the change of demand.

As a supplementary to the earlier Committee's recommendations the Vaghul Committee suggested measures to improve the call money market, commercial paper market, government paper market, as also the development of new institutions and instruments. The Working Group pointed out that in a dynamic market environment, there would be continuous development and refinement of instruments and the monetary policy would be more effective.

On the recommendations of the Working Group and the Narasimham Committee[4] many steps have been taken to develop the money market by setting up new institutions and introducing new agencies. As stated above, the objective has been to develop competitive financial market structure free from government command and control and social inhibitions in which individual corporates and government will have a level playing field.

(a) To evolve this structure a set of new institutions have come up in the money market. The most important are the Discount House of India (DHI), the Money Market Mutuals (MMM) and the Security Exchange Board of India (SEBI) as also the National Stock Exchange (NSE). These institutions in the primary and secondary markets have important implications for call money market, debt market, foreign exchange market and the secondary market.

Since its inception in April, 1988 DFHI has been very successful in promoting the treasury bill market. Its turnover in treasury bills and in inter-bank call and short notices has been extensive. Besides, it has also been operating in the secondary market of commercial papers (CP). After the reorganisation of Treasury Bills market, discussed latter, the DFHI has brought about sufficient flexibility in the flow of liquidity in the bill market.

Another astounding development is the emergence of mutual funds which have grown both in size and importance. Beginning with UTI, the financial institutions like LIC, GIC, and important commercial banks (SBI, Indian Bank, PNB, Canara Bank) have started mutual funds through their merchant banking subsidiaries. These mutual funds agencies play important role in mobilising resources and reducing the risk of portfolio investment of small and medium investors. Along with domestic resources mobilisation, offshore funds are also being brought through (a) India Fund (1986) and (b) India Growth Fund (1989) which are listed in major international stock exchanges.

Setting up of Security and Exchange Board, and National stock exchange are important steps in regulating and systematise the operation of the secondary money market.[5] But, in the primary market there has been significant change in structure and dealers as also in operation. The intention of these changes has been to provide sufficient flexibility to the issuers and to strengthen the criteria for accessing the securities of the market. Nationalised banks now have no entry restrictions and they have been allowed to price issues at a premium, with only two years profitability record. Similary, the Housing Finance Companies are considered to be registered for issue purposes.

In the secondary market, the SEBI [Foreign Institutional Investors (FII)] Regulation, 1995 has been amended to allow the FIIs to invest up to 10 per cent in the equity of any company, in debt securities and also in government securities. From 1993-94 FII's investments have increased considerably; of the 427 FIIs registered, on average, about 130 have been active in over 600 scrips.

These institutional changes in Indian money market have important implications for allocation of liquid fund, for stability of the financial system, for interest and exchange rate and, finally, for real economic response. Before we turn to these implications it is important to see other segments of the money market, namely, the call market, the foreign exchange market, the gilt—edged market, and the overall liquidity of the system. The important liquidity sources of the system are the bank liquidity, government treasury bills and the foreign exchange market. The three segments of the money market are associated with these three dimensions of liquidity.

Instruments-wise innovation has been equally prominent in recent years. The Certificate of Deposits (CD) and Commercial Papers (C.P.) are two important instruments for trade in the market. Recently the corporate agencies find it difficult to have long-term bank credit due partly to banks lukewarm attitude to business position and also due to high interest rate. Corporate bodies are therefore seeking permission to float new instruments to raise funds from the market. Recently the FICCI proposed to introduce 21 such instruments (such as zero coupon bonds, floating rate notes, industrial revenue bonds, clip and strip bonds, dual convertible bonds, notes with warrants for debt, indexed floating rate notes, bought out deal, factoring services, forfeiting, book building, forward contract, swaps, financial futures and caps. In due course these instruments may be introduced through the amendment of Companies Act. As for dealing in instruments, banks are now free to invest in CDs issued by other banks and financial institutions, in the secondary market. On the other hand banks are banned from buying public sector bonds in the secondary market which implies that banks are induced to invest in PSU in the primary market.

In the bond market therefore there are array of bonds both issued by government and private sector. Some of such bonds, such as deep discount bonds (DDB) and flexi bonds of IDBI, are very popular for attractive concessions and market capitalisation. Other FIs such as ICICI, IFCI and SCICI's multi-option bonds have also fetched considerable resources from the money market.

Thus the bond market has become vibrant with the participation of multiple agencies, the Government, the PSU, private sector and the foreign institutional investors (FIIs). This has led to a competitive rate of bidding, interest and yield pattern. The most important aspect of these developments in the bond market is that the government and the RBI are only junior agencies and the competition for dominence is going on between FIs and the private sector. We shall see further on this issue after examining the primary market and the foreign exchange market.

The important part of primary market is the gilt-edged market on the line of recommendations of the Chakraborty Committee and Government Treasury Bills have been changed instructure and interest rate. Steps have been taken for a progressive 'marked to market' valuation of government securities. These steps include (a) increasing interest rate, (b) encouraging the banks to hold larger volume of investment in government securities, (c) liquidity support to mutual funds dedicated exclusively to investment in Government Securities, (d) RBI issue of guidelines to banks for retailing of government securities with non-bank clients. In order to make the government securities trading more popular primary dealers (PD) started operating. Besides the (DFHI) and the SICI, four more primary dealers namely, SBI, Gilt Limited, PNB Gilt Limited, ICICI Securities and Gilt Securities Trading Corporations have started functioning as market makers of government securities.

Central and State Governments borrowing and dated securities constitute an important part of the gilt-edged market. The general trend is that RBI involvement in government dated securities is declining and that of primary dealers is rising.

Important changes took place in the field of Treasury Bills. 91-day Treasury Bills and 364-day Treasury Bills are the two very important instruments for resource mobilisation by the government. Until recently the RBI ad hoc Treasury Bills were important source of resource mobilisation by the government; but recently the RBI has reached an agreement with the government for phased reduction of the issue of ad hoc TBs. This continuation of the issue of ad hoc treasury bills and 91-day Treasury Bills to finance the budget deficit of the government and, instead, introduction of a scheme of Ways and Means Advance (WMA) by the RBI to the Central Government is a bold step to reduce the monetization of government deficit and dependence on the RBI. The TB market is an important segment not only for government resource but also for setting right the flow of liquidity, influencing the interest rate and for regulation of the market. The reform process in money market, started with the implementation of Chakraborty Committee's recommendations, has brought about some element of competiveness in the TB market. Now that the interest rate on TBs has been raised, the body of nonetization has been reduced and a set of Primary Dealers have come up to prop up the TB, the gilt edged market is emerging as an effective platform for the RBI to implement the competitive norm for setting interest rate and control. We shall turn to this point afterwards.

The forex market and the call money are very close and inter-linked. Two important issues of call money market are the call rate and the participants. On both these counts important changes took place; ceiling on call money rate has been relaxed and the new participants of non-bank financial intermediaries like LIC and GIC have joined. Freeing interest rate and participation of intermediaries have changed the character of call money market and it has brought about more flexibility and liquidity in the market. However, at times, the call money market shows unusual and violent gyration which results in problems for the RBI.

As a part of the call market, the foreign exchange market also reflects instability due to various national and international factors. The flow of foreign exchange from current and capital account of the balance of payment has important bearing on the call market and availability of liquidity. However, in both the overnight call market and foreign exchange market the RBI inter vention has an important bearing. Liquidity in these markets come from foreign trade and capital, bank, government and the RBI. Inter-bank call money rates often reach to a very high level of 100 per cent as in 1995 and again fall to as low level as less than 1 per cent (in March-April 1997), depending upon funds released from RBI operation and foreign exchange market as well as from government borrowing and deposit growth. Over the last two years or so inflow of foreign capital being moderate liquidity demand in the foreign exchange market had to be controlled through the manipulation of foreign exchange requirements of exporters and importers and through banking regulation.

Reform in the banking system has two important influences on deployment of fund. On the one hand, the prudential norms inforcement has made the banks and financial institutions alert about their viability and on the other, made then alarmed of the credit expansion and non-performing assets. With the high growth of deposit and low return on securities and low demand for loans, banks are now flush with fund which is further increased through the reduction of CRR and SLR. However, this growth of domestic resources is balanced by moderate flow of foreign exchange. The foreign exchange market and call market therefore remained saddled with plethora of resources for quite sometime. The problem of the financial market is finding the appropriate channel for use of fund which the market fails to show. There are two channels of the use of liquidity, one is the profitable channel of industry and activities which the market process will direct, and the other is the discretionary programme for socially desirable activities. In the present state of our financial market liberalisation, the first channel has become a blind alley and the second channel has become benumed and the government is indulged in borrowing only to compensate its revenue shortfall to which we shall turn latter.

II. IMPLICATIONS AND LIMITATIONS OF TRANSFORMATION

The objectives of financial liberalisation and the measure taken towards that direction, as examined above, have some important implications.

(1) The money market has been extended through setting up of new institutions and introduction of new instruments. It has introduced in-house competition among the markets and agencies but not necessarily led to optimal use of resources.

(2) The promotion of interest rate flexibility outside the command of the authority was the most important recommendation of the Chakraborty Committee. However, the present move of market-Oriented liberalisation of the financial sector has not brought about the desired result. Instead, in the interest rate structure there is neither any uniformity nor sufficient flexibility. There are at present more than a dozen interest rates and this diverse rates act against each other. Nor the RBI bank rate has become a rallying point as a relevant reference rate. The mismatch in the rate structure has reduced the institutional and allocative efficiency as the market rate refuse to decline. As at present there is neither market clearing interest rate nor an evolving relevant reference ratey, the fragmented money market remained as distorted as ever. However, an integration of money, foreign exchange and government securities market is taking shape, all to the interest of money brokers.

(3) This interest rate stickiness has set a cost barrier to the financial institutions and corporates for investment. Besides the limping administration, gloomy profit expectation has gripped the market in which credit flow to the industrial activities is sluggish even as the banks are flush with funds.

(4) Given the evolving grid of money market, foreign exchange market and the government securities market together, the traditional dichotomy of Indian money market is getting further accentuated. Already the priority sector-lending is declining, and the current trend of shyness of financial institutions will slow down the real activities further.

(5) On the contrary, money flow began to be robust towards

the speculative activities. Already the foreign banks have began cross-border arbitrage of foreign exchange, now that the forex market is showing subdued trend with the RBI intervention and slow interest of FIIs.

(6) An important implication of our emerging money market is the gradual integration with the global capital market. As mentioned above, foreign investment in Indian securities is taking place through the issue of Global Depostory Receipts (GDRs) and Foreign Currency convertible Bonds (FCCBs). Besides, Indian Euro Issues, the FII's part-folio investment has imported a new dimension in Indian money market. Various concessions to NRI deposits and investment are also increasingly appearing in Indian money market. (7) As it appears, the emerging money market in India is increasingly being effected by brokers, dealers, and foreign banks operating in India. Their influence through foreign exchange market has become more clear in recent years. The RBI's continuing elbowing in either market is a clear indication of this tenaceous course in which occasional shocks developed by different sporadic and even deliberate factors, such as scams in domestic front, are generating instability. (8) But what is about the monetary policy? One of the objectives of the money market reform, as mentioned above, was the efficient and effective application of the monetary policy of the RBI by making itself free from the dependence on the government. However, while the ad hoc TB has been replaced by WAM, the market borrowing of the government and the monetisation of the dated securities remain. The monetary policy of the RBI for from being target-oriented will itself be the target of invisible forces of inter-national and national market. Thta the distortions have already developed is clear from the diverse credit flow and the consequent slow down of real activities.

What are then the limits and limitations of the emerging Indian money market? The conclusion is inescapable that our money market reform has extended the horizon to the international level and our incipient urban money market is being manipulated by powerful forces beyond the control of the RBI. The limitations of this money market transformation are that (a) rural money market has been totally neglected, (b) majority of producers in the economy, namely, small entrepreneurs and priority sectors are being increasingly, marginalised, (c) and the discretionary regulations are repidly being eroded and distorted.

III. MONEY MARKET REFORM THAT MATTERS

The over hauling of Indian money market is long overdue. But it did not take place in full length even though the revolutionary teps were taken with the nationalisation of the commercial banks. Although financial institutions were multiplied the integration of dychotomized Indian money market remained outside the agenda. The present market-oriented reform aiming at eliminating the financial repression has again bye-passed the rural sector wherefrom the target volume of GDP comes.

Why the present financial refrom is decoupling the financial economy from the real economY?[6] This is because the money market reform started with a distorted view of the economy. With profound structural distortions in the economy with respect of production and finance, the monetarist reform plan, as dictated by neo-classical doctrine, only emphasised on the monetary target without considering the perspective of productions. Money market reform, under such structural backwardness should be preceded by production plan.

At this stage the rural reform should be the begining of the process. Rural money market plan would be aligned with rural production plan. Instruments of the rural financial market should be such that their creation and marketability in the secondary market should be connected with the urban money market so that liquid fund of the money market really flows down to the real production level. The present emerging money market is evading this stage and the money multiplier is taking place without generating corresponding income.

Money market reform, in the first leg, must formulate the structure of rural financial institutions and also the plan for financial instruments that may correspondingly develop in the rural sector, consistent with the rural production plan. In the second stage, these rural institutions and instruments are to be aligned with the urban sector for further support. This process will develop rural-urban financial flow and the money market integration of the rural and urban segments will provide the necessary strength to absorb the shocks of uncertainty and risk. More of credit flow to the productive enterprises should be the first objective of the money market reform. While the emerging money market is freeing the finance for dealers in stock brockers, it is discouraging for the productive enterprises to venture in innovation and investment due to in-built instability and escalating cost. As stated above the elimination of financial repression and development of competitive effeciency require large number of enterprises to play the game; otherwise the unequal competition will result in imperfect distribution of resources to the profit of a few strong players in the market. This calls for an activist and regulatory government in a structurally backward economy like India. This is essential for healthy competition to develop as well as different disadvantaged sectorss of the economy to grow up and to participate in competitive game. A developed money market comprising the urban and rural sector will surely act as stimulant in the investment decision. It requires a radical restructuring of entire financial institutions and innovation of instruments applicable in different sectors of the financial market. Integration of call money market, foreign exchange market and the government securities market opens the tunnel for liquidity to outside or speculative activities in share market rather than promotion of real activities. To do that wider integration of rural-urban financial channel is essential so that larger production can match with wider financial base.

IV. CONCLUSION

Radical measures are taken to transform the Indian money market from a closed, inward and narrow domestic space to the open, outward-looking in which financial units, national and international, can have competitive and efficient operation for optimal gain. In order to climinate financial repression interest rates have been free at certain level of bank deposit and lending, foreign financial institutions have been allowed to invest in domestic capital market and domestic financial institutions to operate in global capital market, securities market has been reorganised with the setting up of new institutions (like DFI and Primary Dealers), introduction of new instruments (like CP, CD) and new organisations (like NSE). Money Market, government securities market and the foreign exchange market have been clubbed together in a closer grid which has been integrated with global capital market.

This grand scheme of liberalisation and globalisation of money market and capital market has brought to the fore many distortions without necessarily enhencing efficiency of institutions and allocation of resources. Money market instability is occasional with call rate either at 100 percent (1995) or at less than 1 percent (1997); foreign exchange market is fed by NRI and portfolio capital flows rather than by genuine trade earnings; credit delivery to the productive sector, industry or agriculture, is tardy whereas banks and financial institutions are flush with liquidity.

There is hardly any possibility of evolving a relevant reference rate inspite of the prevalence of a more than dozen. interest rates. Financial deepening has brought about a plathore of finance companies with projects of doubtful relation with production. Emerging money market is increasingly decoupling the financial sector from the real economic activities rather than diverting the flow of fund to the priority and vast number of small enterprises.

In our dualistic economy where the rural sector dominetes, money market reform should start from reorganising rural financial structure, both institutions and instruments, so that fund can sufficiently flow to the wider activities and occasional shocks can be absorbed. In doing this government has important role for regulation and redirection of competitive financial institutions evolving under the regime of liberalisation.

References

Reserve Bank of India (1985); The Committee to Review the Working of the Monetary System. (Chakraborty Committee).

———, (1987); *Report of the Working Group on the Money Market.* (Vaghul Committee).

Shaw, E.S. (1973); *Financial Deepening in Economic Development*, Oxford, London.

Government of India (1991); *Narasimham Committee Report on the Financial System.*

———, (1996);*Economic Survey*, 1995-96, 1996-97.

Majumdar, NA, (1996); 'Financial Sector Reforms' *Economic & Political Weekly*, March 23.

Index

Allen, 155
Amanulla, 62
Analytical Structure, 62
Assets and Liabilities of all Scheduled Commercial Banks, 1992-93, 80
Asset Liability Management, 11
Attri, V.N., 137

Banerjee, Amalesh, 196
Bank for International Settlement, 13
Basu, Sanjib Chandra, 86
Behaviour of Money Market Rate and Real Interest Rates in India, 1960-1991, 143
Bergh, Van den, 57
Berthelemy, J.C., 138
Bhide, M.G., 3
Bhoi, B.K., 88, 176
Bionomial Probit Model, 130
Brillinger, 89
Broad Money, 140
BSE Sensex of Share Prices, 68

Capital Issues in the Primary Market, 69
Capital Market in India,
Role of Commerical Banks, 75
Cash Reserve Ratio, 26, 183
Central Settlement Agency, 9
Certificate of Deposit, 51, 151, 153, 168
CDs in the London Money Market, 154
US CD Market, 154
CDs in the Indian Money Market, 155
Chakraborty, A.J., 75
Chakravarty Committee Report, 1985, 14, 45.
Changes in Indian Money Market, 197
Chari, Vijay Laxmi, 151
Chatarath, 62
Chatterjee, P., 196
Collier, Phillipine, 117
Commercial Banking System, 18
Commercial Bills Market, 49
Commercial Papers, 50, 169
Committee on Capital Account Convertibility, 5
Comparison of the Auto-regressive Structure and Testing of the Random Walk Process, 92
Credible Yield Curve, 10

Dealing and Settlement Mechanism, 7
Delivery *vs.* Payment, 6
Derivative Usance Promissory Notes, 169

Developed and Less Developed Villages, 124
Developing Countries,
International Bond Issues, 1983 to 1996, 38
International Equity Issues by, 1993 to 1998, 39
Development in the Area of Commercial Banks, 1991, 77
Management of Liability, 79
Management of Banking Assets, 80
Development of Government Security Market, 187
Development of Money Market in a Market Economy, 32
Discount and Finance House of India, 48, 88, 173
Domestic Capital Market, 26

East Asian Economics by Emery, 1992, 57
Economics of Structural Adjustments, 102
Edwards, Sebastian, 139
Emerging Money-Market in India under Economic Reforms, 137, 176
Empirical Facts, 67
Empirical Results :
Area Owned, 125
Share of Leased-in Land in the Total Operated Area, 125
Area, 125
Caste, 125
Education, 126
Proportion of Adult Earning Members, 126
Proportion of Non-Crop Income in Total Income, 126
Per Capita Debt, 126
Ownership of Agricultural Assets, 126
Evolution of Money Markets in India, 45
Extent of Interlinked Transactions in the Informal Credit Market, 123

Financial Liberalisation School, 103
Financial Sector Reforms, 102
Foreign Currency Convertible Bonds, 204
Foreign Exchange Market, 138
Foreign Exchange Reserves of Inflation, 146
Foreign Institutional Investors Regulation, 1995, 199
Framework of Capital Market, 29
Fuller, 89
Functional-cum-Institutional, 19
Functioning of Capital Market, 21
Functioning of Money Market in a Market Economy with Reference, 17
Future of Money Market in a Money Economy, 35

Garai, Subodh Chandra, 86
General Environment, 180
Ghana, Aleem, 116
Ghosh, D.N., 144
Gill, Anita, 114
Government Paper, 52
Gulf War, 33

Handa, 158
Henning, 152
Hicks, 87
Hidalgo, 89
Hongkong Monetary Authority, 10

Implications and Limitations of Transformation, 203
Implications of Reforms on Rural Money Market, 107

Implications of Structural Reforms on Rural Money Market, 101
Implicit Yield of 91 Day-T Bills at Cut of Prices 40-41.
Income and Expenditure of all Scheduled Commercial Banks, 1992-93, 83-84.
Indian Money Market, 48
  Call Money, 48
Inflation in Different Exchange Rate Regimes, 1960-61 to 1996-97, 145
Inter-Bank Participation Certificates, 170
Interest Rate Liberalisation and Money Market Development, 13
Interlinkages in the Credit Markets, 116
International Conference on Money and Finance, 30
Issues Launched, 22

Jenkins, 89
Joshi, Vijay, 147
Jugale, V.B., 101

Kaur, Gian, 114
Kneesaw, 57
Kolmogorov-Smirnov-type, 90
Koopmans, 89
Krishnaiah, 89

Least Developed Countries, 30
Long-run Behaviour of Indian Money Market, 86

Malegam Committee, 68
Market Mechanism, 141
Maximum Likelihood Estimation of Binomial Probit Model, 127
Maximum Permission Bank Finance, 186
Maycock, 154
McKinnon, 141, 197
Metal Box, 65
Mitra, Argya Kusum, 45
MMMFs, 51
Mohanty, Deepak, 45
Monetary and Credit Policy, 5
Monetary Indications, 1960-61 to 1974-75, 142
Money Market, 152
Money Market and Foreign Exchange Market, 139
Money Market Instruments, Case of Certificate of Deposit, 151
Money Market Mutual Funds, 7, 47, 170, 177, 190
Money Market Rates, 159
Money Market Reform that Matters, 205
Murty, 62

Narasimham Committee Report, 1999, 76, 144, 176, 198
National Stock Exchange, 198
Nationalised Banks, 1992-93, 81
Nation-wide Market, 8
Nature and Extent of Interlinkage of Agrarian Credit Markets, 114
Nayak Committee, 1992, 106
Need for Reforms, 167
Net Market Borrowings of Central Government, 32
New Economy Policy, 1991, 75
Non-Bank Finance Companies, 12
Number of Households Borrowing, 119
Number of Households Involved in Various Types of Interlinked Credit Transactions, 120-21

Open Market Operation, 187
Ordinary Paid-up Share Capital, 24
Overview of Indian Money Market, 177

Patel, I.G., 144
Percentage of Agricultural Borrowing, 108
Permitted to Operate as Lenders, 192
Policy Changes, 64
Policy Implications, 71
Prices of Capital of Consumer-durable Goods, 28
Public Policy in India, 5

Quarterly Turnover on the BSE, 70

Raj, Dev, 17
Rangarajan, C., 34
Rao, T.V.S. Rammohan, 61, 71
Radcliff Committee, 104
Recent Changes in Money Market, 167
Reddy, Y.V., 34
Reforms in Operation, 104
Reforms in the Government Securities Market, 194
Regional Rural Banks, 114
Relative Rates of Return in Major Financial Markets, 157
Report of the Working Group on the Money Market, 1987, 163
Repo Transactions, 53
Repurchase Agreements, 7
Restrictions Placed by the Regulatory Environment, 12
Role of Money Market, 46
  Players and Instruments, 47
  Patterns of Money Market Development, 47
Roy, Tuli, 167

Schmoiders, Gustav, 104
Secondary Market, 23
Security Exchange Board of India, 198
Security Trading Corporation of India, 179
Segment-Specific Issues, 181
  Call Money Market, 181
  Term Money Market, 183
  Money Market Mutual Funds, 184
  Commercial Papers, 185
  Certificate of Deposit, 186
Self-Help Groups, 106
Seventh NAM Summit, 1983, 30
Siamwalla, 116
Sinusoidal Pattern, 89
Socially Responsible Market Economy, 34
Sodhani, O.P., 183
Srinivasan, 115
Standard International Accounting Practices, 82
Stock Exchanges, 23
Stock Market Adjustments to Policy Changes, 61
Stock Market Indicators, 43-44
Stock Price Determination, 63
Structural Changes,
  Impact of Post-Liberalised Economy, 87
Swaminathan, 115

Tambe Working Group, 163
Tarapore Committee, 145
Term Money, 51
Transformation of Indian Money Market, 196
Treasury Bills, 52
  14-days Treasury Bills, 171
  91-days Treasury Bills, 171
  182-days Treasury Bills, 172
  364-days Treasury Bills, 172
  Institutional Building, 172
  Remaining Lacunae, 174
Trends in Money Market:
  Call Money Market, 53
  Commercial Paper, 54

Certificate of Deposit, 55
91-Day Auction Treasury Bill, 55
364-day Auction Treasury Bills, 55

Univariate Time Trend, 89
Upadhyay, V., 167

Vaghul, N., 30, 155
Vaghul Committee, 30, 156
Vaghul Working Group, 1987, 45, 176
Varoudakis, A., 138
Verma, Neera, 137

Watts, 89
Ways and Means Advances, 201
Working of the Monetary System, 25